**Accounting and
computer systems**

Accounting and computer systems

H. D. CLIFTON, BSC, MBCS
Principal Lecturer in Business Information Systems
The Polytechnic, Wolverhampton

T. LUCEY, MSOC SC, FCMA, J DIP MA, MBCS
Principal Lecturer in Business Studies
The Polytechnic, Wolverhampton

petrocelli books NEW YORK 1974

ISBN 0-88405-066-1
LC 73-19846

First U.S. edition by
Petrocelli Books, div. of Mason & Lipscomb Publishers, Inc.,
in 1974

Library of Congress Cataloging in Publication Data

Clifton, Harold Dennis.
Accounting and computer systems.

Bibliography: p.
1. Electronic data processing—Accounting.
I. Lucey, Terence, joint author. II. Title.
HF5657.C55 1974   657′.028′54044   73-19846
ISBN 0-88405-066-1

Printed in the United States of America

Contents

Preface

If Fra Luca Paciolo had been able to examine the accounting systems and methods employed in the majority of organisations up to the mid-1950s, he would have been able to easily recognise and understand the records kept. If he carried out the same exercise today he would probably be utterly bewildered. The reason for the abrupt change in comprehension in such a relatively short time has been the introduction of more and more computer-based accounting systems.

Not all the conversions have been an unqualified success but, regardless of any short-term problems, computers are here to stay and will inevitably play an increasing part in handling the organisation's data processing requirements.

Accountants as a body have been slow to embrace all the implications of computers, but individual accountants have been well to the fore in developments over the past decade or so. They have controlled and implemented computer systems and have helped to develop a professional approach towards the application of computers, culminating in the election of an accountant, Alex d'Agapayeff, as President of the British Computer Society.

With the growth of specialised facilities and computer bureaux, involvement with computers will increase even for the smaller organisation, thus causing more and more accountants to be closely associated with computers.

The intention of this book is to help to provide students of accountancy and accountants, of whatever specialisation, with a basic knowledge of the way computers can help them, and of the ways they can help to implement effective and profitable computer-based systems.

H.D.C./T.L.

Chapter 1 Accountants and Information Systems

1.1 Accountants and data processing

Traditionally accountants have been pre-eminent in the administration, recording and provision of quantitative information within organisations, and have thus occupied an enviable position of authority. This situation still applies in many areas but there are increasing pressures from other groups such as systems analysts, business school graduates, operational researchers and management scientists to take over a considerable part of the accountant's function particularly the provision of information for planning, control and decision making.

Because of the accountant's position in the structure of the organisation and the large amount of repetitive work involved in the recording aspects of the accountant's function a natural progression was for the accountant to take charge of the mechanisation of record keeping. This tendency was particularly pronounced in the early stages when keyboard accounting machines and punched card equipment were being generally introduced.

To a lesser extent the same tendency was apparent upon the introduction of computer-based data processing systems (d.p. systems), and consequently in a number of organisations the accountant found himself in charge of d.p. systems, and in many organisations is still in control.

Regrettably, the situation has not reflected entirely to the credit of the accountants. The consulting firm of McKinseys have conducted two famous surveys [1, 2] in the United States covering a wide range of computer installations and the following quotation from the earlier survey expresses a viewpoint prevalent among systems people,

'... unlike the average companies, where computer systems managers' backgrounds are confined entirely to accounting, systems managers in the lead companies have typically had extensive systems experience, supplemented in some cases by operating experience as well.'

These and similar findings are not confined only to American experience and conditions. A recent survey [3], conducted by the P.E. Consulting Group in Britain, gave as one of their conclusions the following:

'Management-services-based d.p. departments appeared to be more success-ful than accounts-based departments. They also had a wider scope of appreciation and reported at a higher level in the management structure.'

The alternatives facing accountants

It can, of course, be argued that most accountants do not want to become managers of d.p. departments so that the implied criticisms in the quotations above apply only to a minority. To the extent that accountants need not become managers of d.p. departments this argument appears superficially attractive. However, this is not coming to terms with the current situation.

Increasingly, accountants are coming into contact with d.p. systems either as managers of d.p. departments, users of computer produced reports, suppliers of inputs to the d.p. system, designers or collaborators in the design of d.p. systems, or as auditors of d.p. systems. This means that the accountant must have a more than superficial knowledge of data processing and an awareness of its potential, limitations and difficulties becomes a vital part of a good accountant's knowledge.

If accountants as a group are not prepared to assimilate the new skills required, the other groups mentioned previously will undoubtedly absorb a major part of the work which has until recent years been uniquely associated with accountants. In the face of these new demands and pressures accountants have two alternatives. They can either duck the challenge and relinquish their position or they can prepare themselves for the challenge of the new technology and thus maintain and enhance their position.

The first alternative is clearly unthinkable yet the response by the Profes-sional Institutes was belated.

Happily the situation has improved dramatically over the past few years and now data processing and systems knowledge is included in the syllabuses of the main accounting bodies, the Institute of Chartered Accountants, the Institute of Cost and Management Accountants, the Association of Certified Accountants, and the Institute of Municipal Treasurers and Accountants. All of these Institutes have produced publications [4, 5, 6] on particular aspects of data processing and they promote seminars, study groups and research projects.

There is therefore a real and growing awareness that all accountants, whether in public practice, in industry or in local or central government must become familiar with the application, installation, control and auditing of d.p. systems. This book has been written with the objective of providing accountants with enough knowledge of the various facets of data processing to be able to fulfil their primary role of accounting in its broadest sense, whilst taking full advantage of the opportunities which are possible in d.p. systems.

1.2 The accountant's contact with data processing

It is conventional to consider that data processing will impinge on the work of accountants in three main ways:

1 The transfer on to d.p. equipment of so called 'routine' applications and record keeping. These applications are often under the control of the accounting function and typical examples are personal ledgers and payroll.
2 The provision of planning, control and decision-making information by d.p. systems. In the jargon such systems are termed Management Information Systems (MIS).
3 The impact that (1) and (2) above have on the work of the auditor, whether external or internal.

These divisions are to a large extent arbitrary because the three areas are indivisible and decisions made concerning any of them may have repercussions on the others.

In addition to the three categories of involvement outlined above the accountant, as d.p. manager or financial adviser, is also likely to be concerned with data processing in the following ways:

1 Decisions on the financial case for the installation of a d.p. system.
2 Decisions on the financial case for the transfer of new applications on to an existing computer.
3 The control of day-to-day computer operations.
4 Liason with systems personnel on systems investigations and design.
5 The periodic review of costs and benefits of the d.p. system.

The detailed implications of these involvements are covered in subsequent chapters but to set the later material into perspective it is necessary to first discuss some general considerations relating to d.p. systems.

Routine applications

This description is normally used to describe applications such as invoicing, ledger work, payroll, and costing analyses; a high proportion of computer applications falls into these categories as has been discovered by various surveys [7].

Accordingly, these are areas of importance not only in their own right but as a basis for more 'advanced' applications. It is fundamental truth of data processing that the development of computer-based MIS cannot proceed without the basic procedures and record keeping of the organisation being under computer control. Because of the significance of these routine applications it is better to term them Foundation Applications to show clearly their over-all importance in the development of d.p. systems in the organisation.

Rather than attempt to distinguish, somewhat artificially, between the data processing associated with foundation applications and the provision of management information it is better to recognise the close relationship that exists and consider the over-all system as flows of information and decisions as shown in Fig. 1.1.

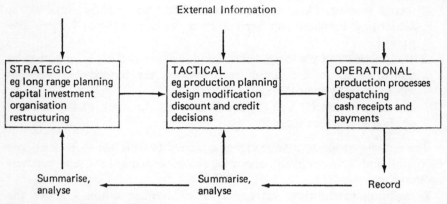

FIG. 1.1   Information flows

From Fig. 1.1 it will be apparent that the information for management planning and decision-making at the various levels stems, in part, from the foundation applications of the organisation. The process of recording operational transactions, in quantities, weights, times, and values, creates a sound data-base upon which the subsequent information system rests.

Accountants have long been accustomed to providing a partial data-base for the organisation's information system. This has been in the form of the familiar sales and purchase ledgers, cost and production records, credit and payment records, variance analyses, etc., instead of computer-maintained files which, although containing the information previously recorded, are usually more comprehensive in their scope and therefore usefulness.

Automatic decision-making

There is an increasing tendency for more and more tactical and operational decisions to be made automatically, i.e. a decision upon a situation will be made by the application of a predetermined decision rule, usually in the form of a simple formula or a series of logical tests and comparisons. A typical example might be the determination of the credit status of a customer which can be shown in the form of a flowchart as in Fig. 1.2.

The tendency for more and more tactical and operational decisions to be made automatically can be advantageous in that decisions can be made

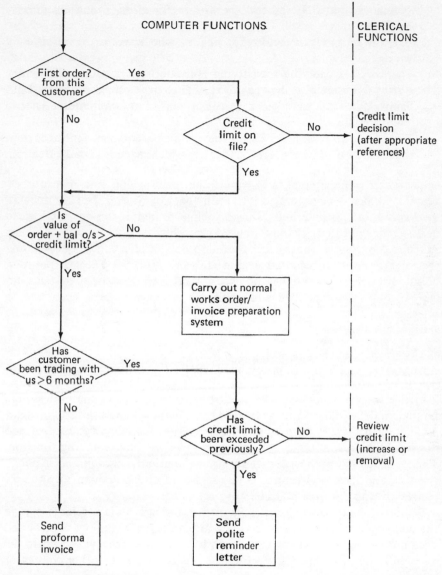

COMPUTER FUNCTIONS.

CLERICAL FUNCTIONS

First order? from this customer — Yes

No

Credit limit on file? — No

Yes

Credit limit decision (after appropriate references)

Is value of order + bal o/s > credit limit? — No

Yes

Carry out normal works order/ invoice preparation system

Has customer been trading with us > 6 months? — Yes

No

Has credit limit been exceeded previously? — No

Yes

Review credit limit (increase or removal)

Send proforma invoice

Send polite reminder letter

Fig. 1.2   Credit status test

consistently in accordance with the prescribed decision rule or test. However, a number of aspects need attention to ensure that the practice is beneficial and that the decisions made are relevant and appropriate to current circumstances.

1 The decision rule, formula or tests must be appropriate to the objectives of the particular facet of the system in which the decision criteria are employed. It should be noted that these objectives will be specified not by

systems analysts, but by the line and/or functional managers directly involved.

2 There is no merit in consistency *per se*; who wants to be consistently wrong?

3 There must be continual monitoring of the decision rules embodied in the system to ensure that they can deal with current situations. Changes in habits, amounts, timings or methods may make yesterday's criteria inappropriate.

4 There is the absolute necessity for the routine system to recognise the non-routine item or situation, that is, the item which requires human attention.

The latter point is a restatement of the fundamental rule of exception reporting which is incorporated into many control systems, be they manual, mechanised or computerised. This principle of not reporting but instead dealing automatically with those transactions which conform to plan, is ideally suited to d.p. systems provided that an appropriate plan can be devised, and the points given above regarding decision rules are observed. The incorporation of automatic decision-making and exception-reporting into d.p. systems has the two fold advantage of dealing with the majority of items according to management's plans yet conserving valuable managerial time to deal with the really tricky situations.

1.3 Management information systems [MIS]

To judge from the literature on accounting, the contents of the professional journals and the changes that have been made in the syllabuses of all the major accounting bodies, the provision of information for planning, control and decision-making is a major and increasing part of the accounting function. This is particularly pronounced in the industrial field but accountants in public practice, and local and central government are also becoming increasingly concerned with this area of accounting activity.

Similarly, the provision of management information plays a large part in the philosophy of d.p. systems and the availability of planning, control and decision making information appears to be one of the decisive factors in the decision to install a d.p. system. Clearly, this is an area of either conflict or mutual co-operation.

Before any attempt is made to discuss MIS, it is as well to define what is understood by this term. There are, of course, as many definitions as there are writers but a reasonably comprehensive definition would seem to be the one quoted by Bridgman and Green [8]:

'It is an information system making use of available resources to provide managers at all levels in all functions with the information from all relevant sources necessary to enable them to make timely and effective decisions for planning, directing, and controlling the activities for which they are responsible.'

It will be noted that no mention is made of d.p. systems or any other means of processing information. This is as it should be. The emphasis, rightly, is on the uses to which the information is put and not on the means of processing that information.

It must be realised that, whatever definition is used, any system only incurs costs. That is, it has no intrinsic value of its own. It cannot be emphasised too strongly that the *value* of an MIS can come *only* from the *users* of that system and not from the producers of the information.

The users, i.e. management at all levels and functions, can only cause value to be attributed to the MIS as a result of actions following decisions taken using the information provided.

The values which may be imputed to any MIS can only come from actions which,

1 Increase profits.
2 Reduce costs.
3 Utilise resources more effectively.
4 Increase sales.

or in some way increase the present or future operational efficiency of the organisation.

Continually ask the basic question 'Does the system merely produce records of results more quickly, or is it instrumental in affecting the results?'

Because of these considerations the accountant should be extremely wary of justifications for any information system which includes phrases such as 'Managers will receive more information', or 'information will be produced more quickly'. These statements, although ostensibly appealing, do not answer the really important question, 'Will the increased amount of information, the more timely information lead to effective actions?' If not, the only thing we can say with certainty is that the production of the information will incur costs.

MIS reports

The way that information reaches managers from the computer-based MIS is by way of a wide variety of analyses, statistics, summaries, operating statements and so on which can be generally referred to as reports. These reports may be classified into three broad types:

1 Reports providing passive background information. These are often produced at fairly lengthy intervals, in many cases long after the transactions involved took place. Accounting examples are asset records and depreciation summaries.

2 Reports which provide control information to influence and guide current and short term tactical and operating decisions. Accounting examples are, cost variance reports, credit control information, and working capital statements.

3 Reports which provide statistical data for forecasting, corporate planning and longer term strategic decisions. Accounting examples are, investment appraisals and budget models.

It will be apparent from the definition given and the examples of reports produced that some form of MIS exists in all organisations regardless of whether they have a d.p. system or not.

What the computer has made possible is the installation of larger, more comprehensive MIS which service more effectively organisations of growing size and complexity.

It would be less than honest not to admit that very considerable difficulties are being encountered in the introduction of all-embracing computer-based MIS, but some organisations are achieving success however. A particular problem with an MIS is to create and maintain management interest. The enthusiastic support of management at all levels is necessary to ensure that the MIS will be effective and will develop with the organisation. The active participation of management in the planning, design and implementation of an MIS is necessary to avoid a 'them' and 'us' situation developing. The development of a computer-based MIS is likely to affect the accountant's role of interpreter to management. Whereas with previous processing methods further analysis, consolidation and decision making were necessary after the initial data was processed, much of this work becomes unnecessary because of the decision-making abilities, speed and power of the computer. If the accountant is not to be bypassed to some extent, then vigorous participation at all stages in the development of an MIS is essential.

An example of a company that is able to report considerable progress in the development of an MIS is Roussel Laboratories, who have installed an MIS to provide integrated production control and accounting information [9]. The system, built round the concept of exception-reporting, provides 'regular reports', as well as 'request reports' which give more detailed information on adverse performances measured against standards and budgets so that remedial action can be taken more quickly and effectively.

The Management Information and Control System Schematic described by Brinjes and reproduced below in Fig. 1.3 follows the broad pattern of operating, tactical and strategic divisions described earlier in this chapter.

The system depicted in Fig. 1.3 has at its heart the main-stream activities of production planning, inventory management and production control, and the accounting part of the system is merely secondary. This is as it should be, for these main-stream activities are where substantial benefits are to be gained—results will be affected by the d.p. system not merely records of results.

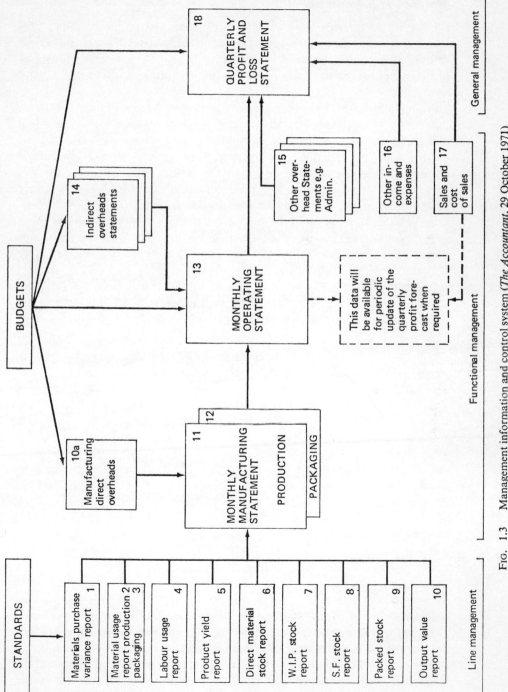

Fig. 1.3 Management information and control system (*The Accountant*, 29 October 1971)

Management functions and MIS

Implicit in the consideration of MIS is an awareness of the functions of a manager and the affect on these functions of an MIS. Again, there are numerous definitions but there is considerable agreement that the manager's functions include planning, control, co-ordinating, implementing, decision-making and motivating.

A computer-based MIS can assist management with some of these functions, but it is important to bear in mind that informal elements of an MIS—individual and group pressures, ad-hoc decision making, discussions—will always exist and indeed, to the extent that management work through people, the informal elements will arguably be more important. The computer-based MIS will cause a shift from informal to formal communications and will provide a more consistent, and accurate data base derived from the foundation applications. Because this will avoid the duplication of records which inevitably exists under manual systems, the computer-based MIS, subject to the provisions described below, should aid co-ordination and increase the likelihood of more effective decisions being taken.

The provision of information is part of a loop which has been variously termed a control loop, a feedback loop or a servo loop. Typical loops at the various levels—strategic, tactical and operating—are shown in Fig. 1.4. This

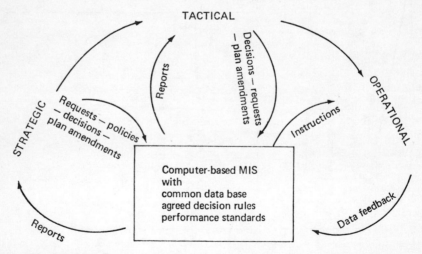

FIG. 1.4 Feedback loops

diagram does not, of course, show the informal parts of the MIS, the personal contacts, the discussions, the bargaining, the motivations which make any MIS, however based, a workable proposition.

The various loops depicted have differing time characteristics. In general the time scale between decision and result, or instructions and result diminishes as one proceeds from the strategic to the operating level. The period of accountability may vary from several years between say, a change in market emphasis implemented by the board of directors, to the foreman being expected to account for variations in performance or wastage on a shift-by-shift basis.

Considerations affecting the implementation of MIS

The implementation of an MIS takes place, in varying degrees of sophistication from the day the first business record is made, perhaps on the back of the proverbial envelope.

Using earlier manual and mechanised methods systems evolved gradually, often with no conscious attempt to consider the real objectives of the system, the implications of the information produced or whether the system was cost/benefit effective.

Because the purchase of a computer and the development of an MIS is a major expenditure and a relatively short time scale is involved, much closer scrutiny is given to the implementation of the new system than ever was given to the old system. Such a scrutiny is, of course, wholly commendable and the financial implications of the examination are dealt with in detail in Chapter 8.

Apart from the financial side there are a number of system considerations that have general application and which are crucial in the development of an effective MIS.

Foundation applications

The foundation applications—ledgers, payroll, costing, invoicing, etc.—must be well designed and acceptable to users in terms of quality, efficiency, and accuracy. The foundation applications are mainly at the operational level and provide the data base on which subsequent developments take place. The basic operations of the organisation must be under control, and the d.p. system catering for them should be well established and an integral part of the organisation's activities.

The human touch

There must be a continuing awareness that computer systems still rely very heavily on people. People provide, code and vet input data and people take actions on computer outputs. There is therefore a need for education at all levels to appreciate the usefulness and, equally important, the limitations of the d.p. system. There is also the absolute necessity for systems designers to appreciate that d.p. systems must support human fallibility over trivial matters and yet not stifle human creativity over non-trivial matters.

Flexibility

Unfortunately, there is a definite tendency for d.p. systems to be more rigid and less capable of rapid change than earlier systems. The most flexible system, though not necessarily the most efficient, is the completely manual one. Because of this inherent characteristic, consideration of the effects of change, possible future developments, and variations in managerial requirements must be a part of systems investigation and systems design. Systems which are open-ended, i.e. capable of expansion without drastic restructuring, are highly desirable although not always easy to achieve.

Participation

There must be active and continuous participation of all interested parties, particularly the management users of the information to be provided. A striking feature of all the surveys of d.p. systems mentioned earlier is that, without exception, in the more successful companies management were fully committed to the concept of data processing and gave active support at the critical times.

Timings

Careful consideration must be given to the turn round time of the d.p. system. There can be an inordinate increase in equipment and design costs to provide information immediately, or with only a short delay, when an analysis of true needs might show that time is not a critical factor. Faster information is not necessarily better information although it will almost certainly be more expensive. The point to remember is that it is the ultimate action which is important and not the intermediate stage of supplying information.

Organisation structures and procedures

Regardless of the implications in the 'glossies' issued by the Computer Manufacturers, an organisation's structures and procedures will not change completely upon the introduction of a d.p. system. Indeed, the tendency to change too extensively in the initial stages should be resisted. There will be enough problems putting basic systems onto a computer without having to cope with substantial changes in the underlying structure and procedures. This is not to say that systems should not change; they should and will. What is wrong is to attempt to restructure the organisation or change the emphasis of functional areas at the same time as the introduction of a new d.p. system. This will almost certainly be too much for most organisations.

Speed of implementation

Closely allied to the point above is the advice to proceed steadily with the computerisation of the organisations systems. Stick to small functional areas at a time and ensure that the systems actually work and are acceptable to the groups affected before proceeding to the next sub-system or functional area. People and organisations can accept change at a limited rate only and too much pressure for rapid change, particularly with a readily identifiable target such as a computer, will almost certainly be counter-productive.

Strategic view of the organisation

Even though one should consider the various functional areas separately for the purposes of implementation, an over-all strategic view of the whole organisations systems and their relationships is a sound planning tool. Typical of such an overview is the one published by the Honeywell Micro Switch Division describing their successful implementation of an MIS.

In 1952 the Honeywell Micro Switch Division commenced system development with the installation of a small punched card system. At that time 58 per cent of deliveries were on time and the sales/stock ratio was 4.3. By 1966 the installation had grown to a medium sized computer and 97 per cent of deliveries were on time and the sales/stock ratio was 6.2. Over-all, this was achieved with an accompanying reduction of the ratio of clerical costs, including d.p. costs, to sales value.

The general flow of information and the main functional areas are shown in Fig. 1.5.

From this original 'total system' outline each function was broken down into major activities. As an example the inventory control function part of the 'Resource planning and Control' box in the total system (Fig. 1.5) is shown in Fig. 1.6.

It will be apparent from Figs 1.5 and 1.6 and the results of the implementation that considerable care must have been taken to ensure that the segments progressively implemented were open-ended and that the system was cost effective at each stage.

Functions and information flows

An organisation is a series of functions linked by information flows as clearly demonstrated by the illustrations above of the Honeywell System.

The design of an MIS should recognise this situation and attempt to deal with the organisation in this manner rather than be completely restrained by existing departmental boundaries. The work done by departments and the divisions of work in existing organisations are often as much due to past pressures, personalities and groupings intended to deal with long-dead situations rather than planned circumstances to deal efficiently with current and future conditions.

The section above outlines some guidelines on the design of MIS and describes some of the pitfalls. Few claims are made by organisations themselves

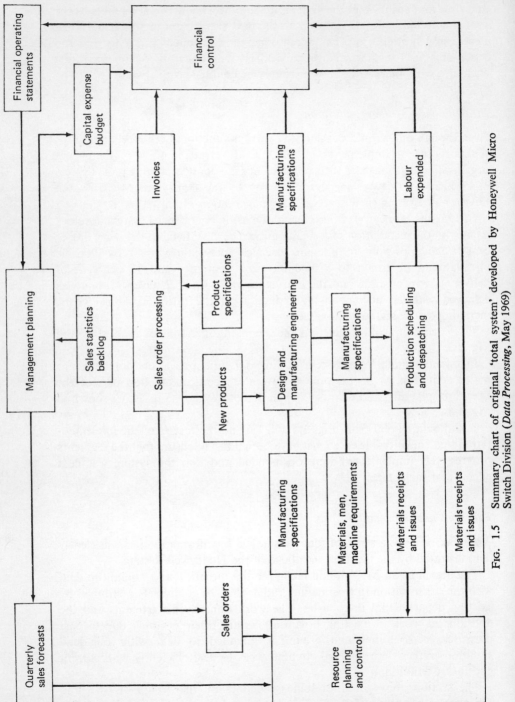

Fig. 1.5 Summary chart of original 'total system' developed by Honeywell Micro Switch Division (*Data Processing*, May 1969)

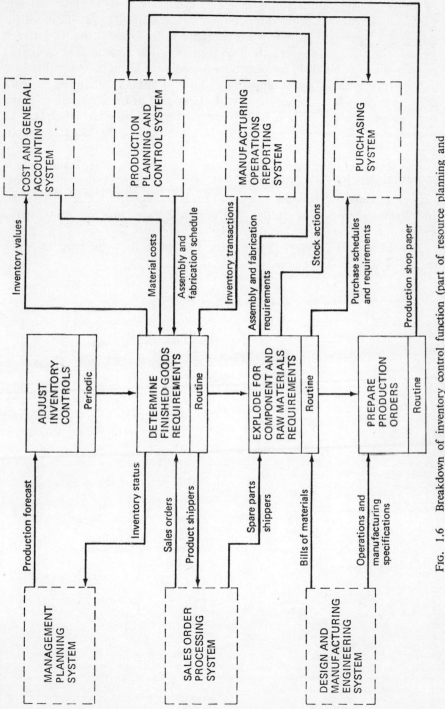

Fig. 1.6 Breakdown of inventory control function (part of resource planning and control) (*Data Processing*, May 1969)

or by computer manufacturers that d.p. systems will be profitable purely based on clerical savings from foundation applications. The justifications for d.p. systems generally include some reference to the benefits that will accrue from the management information derived from the system. It is clear that benefits are possible from better actions based on information supplied by a d.p. system. What is not so apparent is how to quantify these benefits and thereby attempt to make some rational assessment of the likely effect of the installation of a d.p. system. This is clearly an area of vital importance to management and one where the accountant can make a significant contribution.

It is fundamental to remember that the successful computer installation is not necessarily the one with the most up to date equipment, the most sophisticated systems or the one which produces information fastest. It is the installation where the benefits derived from the d.p. system are greater than the costs.

The subsequent chapters of this book attempt to show the ways in which such a system can be achieved.

Chapter 2   Systems Investigation

2.1   The meaning and significance of systems analysis

The term 'systems analysis' is nowadays widely used but nevertheless still has a degree of ambiguity, its meanings within the broad background of industry, technology, science and business are manifold. We are concerned here solely with its significance in connection with business and, in particular, the application of data processing methodology and machinery to business accounting. As can be seen from the succeeding chapters, business systems analysis as an entity embraces a number of functions that are really quite distinct, *viz.* the investigation of existing systems, the study of the information obtained from the investigation, the design and appraisal of a new system, and its testing and implementation. Systems analysis is therefore generic, and so it follows that a proficient systems analyst must be capable of performing all of these functions. The term is also used purely in the sense of studying the findings of an investigation although it is doubtful whether a systems man is eligible for the appellation 'systems analyst' on this basis alone, any more than an accounts clerk qualifies for the title 'accountant' solely because he makes entries in the ledgers.

Why is systems analysis necessary?

In a similar way to many other jobs, systems analysis came into existence simply because a genuine need for such work arose. There has been no definite point of time when this occupation became 'official' since it has, in effect, existed in various forms for as long as mankind has attempted to organise its way of life. None the less we can say that to all intents and purposes the occupation became recognised as such during the early 1960s. Prior to this time, business work was to some extent implemented on computers but this was generally in the form of distinct and isolated applications. Quite often a computerised routine formed only a small portion of the overall application and was in fact completely unconnected with other applications. A typical instance of this situation was the early favourite for computerisation—payroll. Very many firms transferred their payroll routines on to a computer during the early 1960s but generally this was only to the extent of catering for gross wage to net calculations, the build-up of gross wages and the inter-relation of payroll with costing were ignored.

Why was this so? Mainly because the gross to net calculations were easily formulated—in all probability this procedure had been carried out previously for some considerable time by punched card machines. The complexities of gross wage build-up and cost analysis were, on the other hand, such as to require considerable time and effort in order to formulate them for computerisation. Such tasks were at that time likely to extend beyond the responsibilities of one person, section or department of the company. The need to implement more far-reaching applications and to integrate them with one another engendered the demand for persons with sufficient time and ability to be employed solely on these tasks. A number of accountants did at this time take on these duties very successfully but only at the expense of their other work or leisure time. They were for a time carrying out two jobs, and this led many of the more junior accountants to move into full-time systems analysis work.

The stage of development nowadays reached in data processing—sometimes called information technology, necessitates that an over-all view of the firm's activities be taken. Systems analysis now automatically means just this, and whichever business applications are computerised they must connect together in regard to their data input, information output, and their utilisation of the computer files.

Why does the accountant need to know about systems analysis?

The degree of the accountant's need to understand the methodology of systems analysis depends largely upon his proposed level of participation in the tasks involved. If he intends to be employed in the capacity of a computer accounting systems consultant, his knowledge obviously needs to be extensive. On the other hand if he is working in co-operation with full-time systems analysts in the implementation of a new system, his knowledge is essentially the means of facilitating communication with the systems analysts. By the same token, if the systems analyst increases his knowledge of accounting methodology, this will also increase the quality of communication. Idealistically, neither party needs to know the other's job in any way, the accountant would then merely express his problems in logical terms quite regardless of the means of solving these problems, the systems analyst would accept the formulated problem and, after transcribing it into computer concepts, transmit it to the programmer as an abstract notion. This approach has upon occasions worked entirely satisfactorily, mostly as applied to scientific problems where the systems analyst and programmer coped with a problem posed as a set of rules and calculations without their understanding its real implications.

In the business environment this situation does not pertain however; problems and applications do not exist in a vacuum but are closely connected with other problems and with the behaviour of people. Most managers would agree that their jobs would be much easier if human beings were more exactly predictable. It is through the awareness of human unpredictability and of the existence of exceptional circumstances that all aspects of a business application can be encompassed. By understanding the essential features of computer-based d.p. systems, the accountant is in a position to recognise the potentialities of the computer and to anticipate the difficulties likely to arise during the designing and the life of a d.p. system.

The information in the pages that follow is comprehensive enough to meet these requirements, and provides the accountant with a depth of knowledge enabling him to make a positive contribution to the planning of a computerised system.

2.2   The systems analyst

There is no magic in the activities of the systems analyst nor in the workings of the computer he proffers. The mystique of his trade consists for the most part of a mixture of business methodology, common sense and computer technology, the latter tending to be heavily wrapped in the latest computer jargon. Although many other professions possess their own terminology, in very few cases is it so changeable, inconsistent and diffusive as in data processing. The peculiarity of the systems analysts job is that at the moment it is almost undefined in the formal sense, and with the rapidly changing state of the computer world, this absence of formal definition may well be advantageous. A flexible approach to the solution of business problems will be a definite asset in tomorrow's world of data networks and information utilities; yesterday's solutions will become increasingly worthless. Nevertheless, when applying his mind to a particular business application, the systems analyst must have no vagueness as to the objectives and functions of the system he designs. All contingencies should be visualised and catered for, all data precisely labelled, and all requirements met exactly as agreed.

The systems analyst's knowledge and attributes

As with many other occupations, one can prepare a list of the desirable qualities for a systems analyst and finish up with a testimonial for perfection. It is as much the systems analyst's attitude of mind as his education and knowledge that breeds success. Although many systems analysts nowadays have degrees, and this occupation is becoming increasingly filled by graduates, this level of education is not in itself strictly necessary. Within a particular company it is the knowledge of its aims and activities that enables the systems analyst to embark on the best course towards successful systems, and thus the man who has spent some years in a company is at an advantage over the newcomer. At the other end of the scale a person who is deeply entrenched in the formal procedures of an organisation is unlikely to broaden his ideas rapidly enough to be able to design computer-based d.p. systems.

In general terms the knowledge and experience favourable to a systems analyst include:

1 A comprehension of the objectives of the company from the management's viewpoint.
2 The problems and procedures involved in the following applications:
    Financial and cost accounting.
    Stores and stock control.
    Production planning and control.
    Marketing and purchasing.
    Administration—personnel and general.
    Operational research in business.
3 The techniques of d.p. systems design including some familiarity with the problems involved in computer programming.
4 The range of data processing equipment (hardware) currently on the market and its capabilities in relation to costs.
5 The range of application software available and its relevancy to the firm's problems, this applies especially to business application packages.

The responsibilities and duties of the accountant and the systems analyst in the planning of computer-based accounting systems

It is neither sensible nor possible to create a precise demarcation between the responsibilities of the accountant and the systems analyst as related to systems planning. Nor is it possible to specify an exact interface between their duties that would cover all situations in the accounting field because the precise responsibilities of each party as regards the planning of a new system is not absolutely pre-definable. By and large this is a quite satisfactory state of affairs since an overlap of responsibilities results in close discussion of the problems involved, and also creates mutual understanding and appreciation of the other's knowledge and skills. At the same time it is obviously essential that there is no responsibility gap, each person must be fully clear where his liabilities start and finish. Frequent contact and communication between the accounting and systems staff obviate the responsibility gap situation, and also prevent misunderstandings from arising.

It should be remembered that the basic duties and responsibilities of the accountant are not changed by the adoption of data processing methods and machinery. It is therefore encumbent upon him to decide the d.p. system's aims as regards the accounting procedures. As a prospective user of the computer department, the accountant is effectively in the position of being its 'customer', and thus has the right to decide what he wishes to 'purchase'. He should not allow himself to be 'sold' a system merely because it happens to be a convenient one for the computer department staff to implement on the computer.

When the aims and requirements of the system have been determined, it is primarily the systems analyst's responsibility to decide upon the best computer methodology. In some ways he operates as a contact man between the accountant and other users on the one side, and the programmers on the other side. It has been suggested, and not without justification in some cases, that the systems analyst could well be eliminated from this chain of communication since the shorter a communication link the lower is its noise level, that is to say, the clearer and the more accurate would be the information passing from user to programmer. A systems analyst who merely re-transmits a 'photocopy' of other people's idea is of little real use—he must be of sufficiently high calibre to contribute significantly to the design of all applications included in the total system. He cannot be expected however to supersede the prospective user when it comes to deciding the requirements from the system, a logical extension of such a situation would enable the company to be administered by one person only, namely the systems analyst!

It would be most unsatisfactory for each user department within the company to specify its requirements directly to the programmers, this leads to isolated procedures and requirements between departments. As is seen from Chapter 5, a company utilising a computer acquires more beneficial results by creating an integrated system, that is one in which all routines and data are inter-linked in a cohesive manner. It is highly unlikely that this objective could be achieved without someone such as the systems analyst acting as the co-ordinator for all applications in the total system.

Turning for a moment to the programmer, this person by the very nature of his work is extremely close to the detailed programming problems. These demand his attention to such an extent that it is very difficult for him to see a problem through other people's eyes. Whereas for the accountant the problem is, for example, the preparation of the fully correct balance sheet, the programmer sees this as the fitting together of thousands of computer instructions. In other words, most programmers find it difficult to conceive the end product of the system and, in some ways, this capability is unreasonable to expect of them.

The ideal computer man would be the one who fully understands all the applications and who also has a detailed knowledge of programming. He could then write all the programs without referring to other persons, thereby eliminating errors caused by human misunderstandings. We are still awaiting this man's birth so for the present we must manage with what is available! To some extent an analyst/programmer meets the above demands, this is especially so when the range of applications in the system is strictly limited. It has long been a debatable issue as to whether this type of occupation is more efficacious than the two separate posts of systems analyst and programmer, but the argument is not worth pursuing here.

What information must the accountant and the systems analyst provide for each other?

Two minds are better than one—perhaps, but in any event it is certain that nothing is lost by the cross-fertilisation of ideas. The facts of a situation cannot, of course, be ignored but the ideas about it are what really matter. A mere recital of the unadorned facts of a problem almost certainly leads to the adoption of a carbon copy of the solution to a previous similar but not identical problem. Upon occasions this approach is satisfactory, but it is likely to be increasingly less so with the advent of bespoke management information systems and on-line databanks. The accountant can nowadays afford to allow his ideas to have more free rein than ever before because what has previously been inconceivable is now quite likely to be possible. Even if an idea seems fanciful, the accountant should mention it to the systems analyst. The latter is then in a position to balance the advantages to be gained from adopting the idea against the effort needed to implement it—this is part of his job.

What things should the accountant inform the systems analyst about?

1. The results required as output from the system, including both the routine documentation and the special reports. The exact contents of these outputs need to be specified, some of which do not necessarily appear on existing documents. The future requirements of special reports should be forecast as accurately as possible although this task is by no means simple. Even where this forecasting cannot be done with any degree of exactness, it is advantageous to have the appropriate forecasting data available in the computer files and to keep it maintained in an up-to-date condition.

2. The basic input data involved—how much of each type, the constituents of each type, from where it arrives, and whether it is steady in volume, increasing, decreasing or fluctuating.

3. Deadline dates and times, especially those associated with output results and the arrival of input data. The genuine reason for each deadline should be explained so that the systems analyst can decide its pertinancy in the new system. It should be remembered that an existing deadline in a manual system may well disappear by virtue of the system being computerised.

4. The methodology of the firm's accounting routines and particularly any of the more abstruse techniques such as discounted cash flow calculations. It must not be assumed that all terminology has exactly the same meaning to both parties, the possibility of consequent misunderstandings is removed by a careful explanation of the point in question.

5. The ranges of items involved in the firm's accounting activities, the number of items in each range, and their method of sub-division. Connected with each item range is the arrangement and meaning of code numbers, their usage and changeability.

What information can the accountant expect from the systems analyst?

1. The practicability of obtaining a suggested output from the d.p. system. Virtually any output is obtainable but only at a cost in terms of time and money. Solid reasons can be expected from the systems analyst when output is withheld and these should be accompanied by suggested alternatives.

2. A straightforward explanation of the hardware facilities that are currently available together with recommendations regarding their utilisation in new systems. Although strictly the accountant need not concern himself with technicalities, it is of interest to know something about the machinery to be employed and especially that connected with data preparation (Section 3.2).

3. An assessment in user terms of the volumes of data that can be held on computer files for a given cost. The computer's basic storage might not hold all the data that is needed, and so extra cost is then incurred for further storage units. The storing of obsolete or irrelevant data is generally costly both in regard to computer time and the hardware employed.

4. An estimate of the time, cost and effort involved in planning and running each application. The systems analyst will undoubtedly make his opinions known if he believes that a large amount of planning effort is likely to be expended for little worthwhile result. Nevertheless the accountant is in a better position than the systems analyst in deciding the true value of accounting output.

5. An explanation of the additional work likely to be imposed upon the accountant and his staff during the planning, implementation and running stages of the d.p. system. In particular, this work includes: (a) the preparation and vetting of accounting data, both for transference to computer files in the initial stages and later as input to the running system; (b) the allocation and checking of code numbers associated with accounting, e.g. cost heads, account numbers and so forth; (c) the checking of computer output during the early stages of the new system (Chapter 6), and to a lesser extent on a permanent basis.

2.3   Preliminaries to the systems investigation

The most important feature of an investigation is its purpose; initially this might not be as closely defined as is desirable but nevertheless we must set out upon an investigation with some guide lines in mind. Ideally the systems analyst is given an assignment brief by management and this states the objectives of the investigation. In the early stages of considering the potentialities of data processing, the objectives are inevitably somewhat vague, and in order to avoid embarking upon an extensive investigation based on ambiguous objectives it is pragmatic to carry out a brief feasibility survey beforehand. The outcome of this survey can then be used to modify and complete the assignment brief, and this feedback may, if necessary, be repeated several times so that the assignment brief becomes more precise after each cycle of the feasibility survey.

In general terms the objectives of a new system, be it data processing or any other, fall into several categories as well as into long-term and short-term divisions. These objectives might, to some extent, conflict with each other and the responsibility for balancing them falls mainly on the company's management but also on the accountant and systems analyst. It is natural to be concerned more with short-term than with long-term problems, but where these clash with each other, the long-term objectives should obviously be given serious consideration and not merely precluded; to do this might aggravate the planning to be done later.

The categories into which almost all data processing objectives can be separated are as follows:

1 FINANCIAL—the reduction of costs, increase in profits maintenance of budgets etc.
2 INFORMATION—the provision of more accurate, relevant and up-to-date information, particularly for management decision-making purposes.
3 STAFF—a shortage of staff of the right calibre is sometimes a permanent difficulty and this is not necessarily dissipated solely by paying increased salaries to attract new staff.
4 WORK LOAD—this may be increasing steadily or fluctuating to such an extent that an expansion of the existing system would not cope, a new approach must therefore be found.
5 EFFICIENCY—this involves the removal of bottlenecks, increased accuracy, reduced data handling time, elimination of unnecessary work, increased throughput, and a general toning-up of the whole concern.

The steering committee and assignment brief

The assignment brief is the systems analyst's authorisation to carry out a feasibility survey, and subsequently it can be endorsed to authorise a full investigation if circumstances justify this. It should be regarded as a request from management enjoining all staff to assist the systems analyst(s) with the systems investigations. In order to give added weight to the request for assistance, it is usually advantageous for the firm to constitute a steering committee for the purpose of supporting and watching over data processing activities. This committee generally consists of the heads of the departments which would be most affected by the introduction of data processing, together with representatives from the systems department. A senior member of the company acts, for some time at least, as chairman of the steering committee.

One of the first duties of a steering committee is to prepare the assignment brief, modifying it as necessary later in the light of the findings of the feasibility survey. At a later stage in the proceedings, the steering committee decides upon the potential advantages of using a computer, and then acts as the official negotiating body with prospective computer suppliers and service bureaux.

The assignment brief, in addition to acting as an authorisation, provides the systems analyst with the following information:

1 The objectives of the feasibility survey; these should be stated in general terms so that the survey and subsequent full investigation are not confined to within artificial boundaries.
2 The limitations to be imposed upon the survey in terms of locations, applications and work areas. Wherever possible no such limitations should be imposed because by so doing the potential benefits gained from a new system are reduced.
3 References to previous surveys and investigations carried out previously in a similar field within the company.
4 An indication of the maximum capital expenditure or outflow that can be considered. This amount must obviously bear a relation to the savings expected from the new system, and not merely be chosen arbitrarily.

The particular aims of the feasibility survey are:

1 To determine whether the objectives stated in the assignment brief are attainable within the financial and physical (if any) limitations imposed.
2 To expose the major problems existing within the company and thereby to enable the systems analyst to devise his strategy for the full investigation. It is quite possible that these problems were not fully apparent at the time that the assignment brief was prepared.
3 To discover the areas having potential for saving of money, time or effort. These are not necessarily problem areas as such, but are usually those involving high current expenditure and which are therefore open to potential savings.
4 To decide whether specialists will be needed to assist in the full investigation, these people may be drawn from inside the company and/or from outside agencies.
5 To estimate the time and cost of the full investigation, and hence to decide the resources in manpower and money needed to carry it out.

2.4   Procedures of systems investigation

Since in most cases some system or other is already in operation, it is sensible to study this system in depth, so ascertaining not only the facts and figures but also the background to the situation. It is therefore the systems analyst's business to make a detailed investigation of all relevant departments' work, especially in regard to the major routines carried out. As well as gathering a multitude of facts, he is also concerned with ideas and policies; and provided these pieces of information do not become confused one with the other, they can be beneficially combined in the creation of the new system. It is the obligation of all members of the company to provide whatever information they can muster to assist the systems analyst in the investigation. Any objections to a proposed new system should, in all fairness, be raised when the new system is appraised (Chapter 6), and not be allowed to cause distortion or concealment of the true facts appertaining to the existing system.

It is usually the case that the accountant supplies a considerable proportion of the facts and ideas needed by the systems analyst. Where the vast majority of the new system's routines are of an accounting nature, such as in a finance company, it could well be simpler over-all for the accountant(s) to learn about computer systems in some depth than for the systems analyst(s) to fully comprehend the accounting procedures. The logical outcome of this arrangement is for one or more of the company's accountants to take up duty as systems analysts either permanently or temporarily.

What facts does the systems analyst need?

The facts needed from a systems investigation cannot be formed into a neat list catering for all circumstances. It is obvious that the range of facts relating to, say, a stock control situation is vastly different to that appertaining to job costing. None the less we can cover virtually all business applications by acquiring the facts described in Section 2.2 and also under the following general categories:

1 The ranges of items applicable to the company's activities. These are typically the products manufactured and/or sold, components held in stock, persons employed, customer accounts held, cost heads utilised, and so on. In respect of each such range, the required facts are for instance, the number of items, their sub-divisions, code numbers in use, and any special peculiarities of the range of items.

2 The volumes of data dealt with in the company. This includes all documents and especially those received from or despatched to outside agencies.

3 The calculations and logical steps in each routine. These are not generally complicated in themselves but nevertheless it is essential that their precise details are known. For example, the exact method and required accuracy connected with the average pricing of stock issues, although not complicated in themselves, can lead to difficulties if they are inadvertently changed in the new system.

4 The contents and movements of documents. Every entry on each relevant document handled within the company must be clearly identified and understood. By tracing and examining all such documents, the systems analyst obtains a clear picture of the company's activities. In practice a disused copy

of each document, preferably holding live data, is collected for this purpose during the investigation. It is important to remember that the information flow within an organisation is its means of control and stability, and that this flow for the most part takes the form of document movement.

5 The exceptions to the norm. Often the exceptions are the deciding factor in the methodology of data systems. It is also the exceptions that are the most easily overlooked during the investigation. The things to be looked for in this respect are abnormal amounts, special procedures, missing and erroneous data, irregular activities and so on.

6 The organisation and utilisation of staff. By breaking down the departments into suitable groupings, the actual numbers of staff employed and the hours spent on the various tasks can be determined. Since labour costs are normally by far the most significant in office work, this breakdown provides a direct indication of the high-cost activities, thus highlighting the areas susceptible to savings.

How are the facts ascertained?

The main method employed by systems analysts in gathering the facts pertaining to existing systems and situations is simply asking the people concerned. ASKING is backed up by OBSERVING the existing system in action, by MEASURING it, and by READING documents pertinent to it. Whenever possible two or more of these methods should be used in conjunction so as to obtain confirmation of the information received.

ASKING consists mostly of INTERVIEWING the members of staff who operate the present system. This involves the systems analyst in devoting much of his time and skill in eliciting information from a wide range of people.

INTERVIEWING is by no means an automatic process, in some ways it is one of the most skilled of the systems analyst's duties. It is imperative that the systems analyst and the interviewee are at all times in concert during an interview. If the two parties drift on to different courses of understanding when discussing a problem, the systems analyst must be capable of detecting this divergence and should then change his approach accordingly.

Since the accountant is likely to be closely involved in discussions of this nature, the following apposite points are of interest.

1 Prior to the interview both parties should brief themselves on the general situation and on the particular topics to be discussed. It is only too easy to become out-of-date as regards the latest situation even though this relates to one's work.

2 The accountant must have available, either immediately or at short notice, all factual information relating to existing accounting procedures. This again may not be as straightforward as appears at first, information is easily mislaid and creeps unobserved into obsolescence over the years.

3 When information is more conveniently obtained from the accountant's

staff, the appropriate persons should be indicated to the systems analyst and permission given to interview them. It is helpful if the accountant describes briefly the duties and responsibilities of his staff, mentioning any points that might cause difficulty.

4 As well as supplying facts, the accountant also explains the policies applying to his work, and suggests ideas he has for improving the system. Facts and ideas must not be confused however.

5 If the interview is likely to be frequently interrupted by visitors, phone calls, etc., another quieter room is obviously beneficial. Similarly, members of staff called-in to assist should be released immediately they have provided all the help they can give.

6 It is not advisable for the accountant—or any other manager—to sit-in during the interviewing of his staff. This inhibits some persons, and consequently results in distorted and confused answers being given to the systems analyst.

OBSERVING an existing system in action involves the systems analyst in spending some time in each major department or section. To some extent he can participate in the work and in this way become accepted as a member of the department, thereby obtaining a better picture of the true situation. By observing a department in operation certain features are assessed more easily. These include the pressure and spread of the workload, the amount and level of communication between personnel from inside or outside the department or company, the staff's attitude towards the understanding of the present system, and the actual usage of file data by the department.

MEASURING applies both to the items involved and the times taken in the existing system. Items can include virtually anything, from documents to people, and in some instances it is more convenient to apply sampling techniques than measuring the whole of a large range of items. It is quite likely that measuring and counting will be used as the means of verifying a figure given verbally. Measured times include not only those occupied by tasks but also the time intervals between tasks and their effect.

READING documents during a systems investigation should be minimal; this is owing to the relatively large amount of time that this activity takes. This method is, however, useful to the systems analyst when he is given documents such as reports of previous investigations, company instructions and information, selected letters and memoranda. His problem is, of course, selecting the important points from the massive amount of literature presented to him. The accountant and the other prospective users of the new system are in a position to help in this respect.

2.5 Estimating existing system costs

An important part of a systems investigation consists of estimating the costs incurred by the existing system, covering all areas of work that might be transferred on to the new system. The costs should be sub-divided between routines, cost heads and departments in such a way that comparison with the new system is facilitated later. Not only the present costs of the existing system but also those appertaining to the future are of interest; these are likely to change not only with the workload but because of changes to methods and the increasing cost of skilled clerical labour.

Although an analysis of each department's costs is usually available from the company's costing department, the figures therein may not be entirely suitable for purposes of comparison. It is obvious that we must compare like with like, adding further benefits later if necessary, and not merely to compare blanket departmental costs with computer costs since it is unlikely that in reality whole departments will be eliminated. Quite apart from this aspect there is the need to ensure that certain duties of the departmental staff, which are quite outside the scope of the computer, are still catered for in the new system. These include, for example, the answering of queries from customers and suppliers, also other essentially human-contact activities.

A similar argument applies to the usage of office machines; where the apportionment of machine costs depends upon their utilisation by several routines, care must be taken not to apportion a single machine's cost between two or more routines, and then to assume later that this cost is saved pro rata if one of the routines ceased to employ the machine. The rental or depreciation

SALES ORDER OFFICE Staff utilisation in hundreds of hours p.a.				
Routine	Grade			
	A	B	C	D
Order vetting	20	30	150	—
Stock allocation	35	170	40	—
Pricing	—	15	75	—
Extending	—	—	150	—
Invoice typing	—	—	80	140
Ledgers and credit	10	20	65	45
Filing	—	—	20	95
Other work	45	90	60	105
Idle time	—	15	20	35
Totals	110	340	660	420

FIG. 2.1 Staff utilisation table

of that machine is not normally reduced because its amount of use has been reduced.

The first stage in determining existing-system costs is to draw up a Staff Utilisation Table as shown by the example in Fig. 2.1, this table is, of course, constructed from information obtained during the systems investigation. The approximate percentages of time spent by each person in each department on his main tasks are found and converted into hours per week, overtime and additional annual work are added and the result expressed in hundreds of hours per annum. It is important that the staff utilisation table is suitably split up between routines so that these are directly comparable with the computer routines. The segregation of staff into the grades shown is somewhat arbitrary and varies from one company to another, it is intended merely as a means of reducing the amount of calculating involved but should nevertheless provide reasonably accurate figures. One should guard against having too few persons in the highest grade since this might again lead to errors if their salaries were apportioned on a pro rata basis.

The Departmental Costs Table, as shown in Fig. 2.2, is constructed from the

SALES ORDER OFFICE Cost in £ per annum				
	Wages	Machines & Eqpt.	Stationery	Overhds.	Totals
Order vetting	13,400	—	60	2,680	16,140
Stock allocation	19,500	—	25	3,900	23,425
Pricing	5,700	—	40	1,140	6,880
Extending	9,000	1,800	130	2,160	13,090
Invoice typing	10,400	800	3,500	2,240	16,940
Ledgers and credit	8,300	150	900	1,690	11,040
Filing	5,000	450	250	1,090	6,790
Other work	19,500	250	120	3,950	23,820
Idle time	3,800	—	—	760	4,560
Totals	94,600	3,450	5,025	19,610	122,685

FIG. 2.2   Departmental costs table

staff utilisation table together with information regarding other costs such as machines, overheads and stationery. The wages costs are arrived at by multiplying each grade's total hours per annum by the average wage per hour for that grade, and summating the results as shown.

Chapter 3   **Computer Hardware**

3.1   General review of hardware

The information in this chapter is intended purely for the enlightenment of the accountant as an indirect user of data processing equipment, it does not purport to be a detailed description of computer hardware. To attempt the latter against the background of this book would be futile in that there is neither the need nor the space herein. What we are concerned with here is to provide an understanding of computer hardware that (*a*) enables the reader to appreciate its potentialities and, (*b*) gives him some basic knowledge of its technicalities from the systems design aspect. It is of no consequence whatsoever for the reader to understand, for instance, the precise mechanical functioning of magnetic tape units or the electronic circuitry enabling instructions to be obeyed. These points are stressed at this juncture since computer users can easily mislead themselves into believing that a technical knowledge of computer hardware is a pre-requisite to its efficacious utilisation, this is far from the truth.

Essentially the accountant is concerned with three main aspects of hardware:

1 The means by which basic data can be input into the computer for processing.
2 The amount of data that can be held in a computer's storage media, and its level of accessibility.
3 The ways in which the computer can present its output results.

The reason for his need to be concerned with these aspects is simply that they will remain with him for a long time once the d.p. system has become operational. If nothing is known of their characteristics during the system design stage, it is likely to be extremely difficult to make the expedient changes subsequently; even worse, the user might never appreciate that other alternatives are available. It could be argued, and not without some validity, that all this should be left to the systems analyst since he is the specialist and should therefore cover all the possibilities. The possible danger inherent to this attitude is that the systems analyst, because of inexperience of the firm's modus operandi or his over-enthusiasm for computer technicalities, fails to appreciate the advantages or pitfalls of the various approaches to the firm's data processing problems. In respect of systems design, a second opinion, although not necessarily greatly advantageous from the purely technical aspect, often provides the reassurance that the ideas as regards hardware are acceptable to the user.

What is hardware?

In common with most other concocted terms, 'hardware' has a somewhat loose meaning but can safely be taken to mean all physical attributes of computers and associated equipment. Before describing the modern hardware it is worth giving a brief mention to some of the veteran machines associated with the earlier types of computer since some of this are still in use and are likely to be so for some time to come. The particular hardware in mind consists of punched card equipment used with some small computers. These computers cannot store or sort any significant amount of data and therefore are used in conjunction with punched cards and their associated machinery, i.e. sorters, collators and reproducers. A punched card sorter is employed for putting punched cards into sequence and it does this by sorting one digit position at a time into numerical sequence. The maximum rate of sorting in this manner is about 1,000 digits per minute and therefore to sort, say, 10,000 cards into the sequence of a 6-digit number (the key) using one sorter takes approximately one hour—possibly considerably longer if the sorter operator is inefficient. This is much slower than sorting by employing magnetic tape (Section 3.5), but is also much cheaper. A collator is a machine for merging or matching together files of pre-sorted punched cards, it also detects unmatched cards; these attributes make it valuable for preparing files for input to a computer. A reproducer performs two main functions: (*a*) it creates new sets of punched cards from old—as is often needed for computer input, and (*b*) it summarises the results from several cards into the one card. Collators and reproducers are slow devices and are therefore used nowadays only with small files of punched cards.

Hardware in the more modern sense includes the electronic equipment for performing calculations, data storage devices, input and output peripherals, data preparation equipment, data transmission equipment and terminals, and to a lesser extent ancillary machines associated with stationery and other output media.

3.2 Source data media

Every process, event and decision connected with business activities creates source data of some kind or other. All this data might not find its way into computers but that which does must first be transcribed into a form that is comprehendable to the computer's input mechanism. As is well known, computers cannot accept handwriting, ordinary typing or speech as input, and it is unlikely that they will ever do so apart from in the laboratory. It is therefore necessary in practical situations either to transcribe the source data from its original form into an acceptable media or, alternatively, to originate the source data in an acceptable form.

Bearing in mind that source data encompasses a very wide range and that it comes from a multitude of sources, we cannot expect to be able to accommodate it efficiently in only one standard media—desirable as this might be. Since, for instance, documents stemming from a factory environment are unlikely to have had the same degree of care as those from an office, the input media arising therefrom must reflect this in regard to their clarity of layout and their ease of preparation.

Card punching

The universal means of entering business data into a computer was for a long time the standard 80-column punched card, and this is still the predominant medium. Each such card measures $7\frac{3}{8}$ in. $\times$ $3\frac{1}{4}$ in. and is characterised by one of its corners being cut off in order to facilitate the manual handling of packs of cards. A punched card has 80 columns across its width into each of which is punched one, two or three small rectangular holes representing numerals, alphabetic letters and symbols respectively. Various other arrangements of card layout have come and gone in the past, and currently an alternative is the IBM System/3, offering 96 columns of data in a card only one third the size of a conventional 80-column card.

Normally, adjacent columns in a punched card are formed into a field, that is to say any meaningful piece of data such as a quantity, a description or a code number. Fields are consequently of different sizes in a card, but a given field is always the same size and in the identical columns within a set of cards of the same class. There are no absolute positions for fields, the layout of a given class of card is decided entirely to suit its contents and, in particular, the punching of these in relation to the source document from which the card stems. There are literally tens of thousands of different card layouts in current use. Many of the cards are pre-printed with the field layouts and headings.

In order to insert the holes into the cards an automatic punch/verifier is employed. This machine is automatic only to the extent of feeding and ejecting the cards itself, the actual punching of the holes is controlled by means of a keyboard operated manually. The punch operators read the source data from documents and punch the cards' fields a column at a time—somewhat akin to operating a conventional typewriter. This manual punching of cards is a relatively slow, expensive and, to some extent, erroneous procedure, but nevertheless has not as yet been completely superceded by any other method. Following the punching stage the source documents and corresponding cards are passed to another operator who verifies the latter's accuracy by repeating the process but without actually punching any holes. During this verification stage the machine detects any discrepancy between the two operations, and if necessary locks its keyboard so that it cannot proceed until the error has been rectified.

Most punch/verifiers also print across the card's top edge the characters punched, thus facilitating human understanding of its contents; this is known as interpreting and usually the interpretation lies directly above the corresponding column.

Mark sensing

This arrangement obviates the manual punching of cards, instead marks are made manually on the card to represent the data to be entered therein. These small marks must be made laterally using a soft graphite pencil, they are sensed electrically and then converted into conventional holes in the same card by means of a mark-sensing reproducer. A mark occupies the width of three columns of punching, and so 27 marking positions are available across the width of a card. By using both sides of the card, the equivalent of 54 columns of data can be marked and subsequently punched.

Under carefully regulated conditions mark sensing is time-saving, economic and convenient. Unfortunately where ideal conditions do not pertain, this method is liable to incur errors. These are caused by the cards becoming dirty and/or the marks being badly made, both faults resulting in machine-sensing inaccuracies. These difficulties together with a certain degree of conservatism on the part of potential users have prevented the widespread use of mark sensing, and in any case it has now largely been superceded by mark reading (OMR).

Card pulling

As an alternative to the immediate punching or marking of cards to represent current transactions, it is possible to 'pull' or 'pick' cards from a pre-punched file. This is a well-proven method for dealing with a large amount of source data that could not otherwise be dealt with in the time available. The cards in the pulling file are held in special open trays in order to facilitate their rapid selection by the pulling clerks, the cards have been interpreted and the groups appertaining to the items concerned are separated by interspersed label cards.

When employing card pulling in conjunction with a computer's high speed card reader, it is usual to use each card once only; extra data being manually punched into the cards subsequent to pulling if this is necessary. This arrangement is known as a consumable pulling file because the cards have to be replaced after use, and this is usually carried out during slack periods, utilising a reproducer for the purpose. A non-consumable pulling file is one into which cards are re-inserted after use; it is not feasible to punch additional data into these cards and they must be reproduced after a certain amount of use.

A card-per-unit pulling file is one in which the cards represent individual items that actually exist somewhere in the organisation—typically, in the stores. Although this system has diminished in use with the increasing employment of computer files, it has the distinct advantage of providing an immediate indication of the position of, say, the stock level of all items. In dealing with customers' orders received by phone for example, a card-per-unit file shows quite clearly what is immediately available from the stock-in-hand; when orders are received, the corresponding cards are withdrawn from the file.

Card pulling generally has the following advantages:

1 Errors caused by the misreading of descriptions and code numbers on source documents tend to be reduced; this is because the contents of the file give an indication of the indentities of doubtful items.
2 Pulling is faster than punching and verifying, therefore more source data can be dealt with during peak work periods. This obviously depends upon the respective members of staff but, one-for-one, pulling is much quicker.
3 Where the items concerned are from a reasonably static range, as is usually the case, the manual punching load is diminished because a reproducer is employed to punch replacement cards.

The disadvantages of card pulling are:

1 The cards are inherently associated with one type of item only, thus preventing the use of spread cards (see below). Consequently since the cards are not generally filled with data, card consumption and computer card reading time are both greater than for spread cards.
2 The pulling files themselves may occupy a lot of space.

Dual-purpose cards

With this arrangement the punched card itself acts as the source document, data is written by hand on the card itself and subsequently punched manually into the same card. Their use is, for instance, as factory job dockets with some data pre-punched and interpreted before the docket is issued, further figures are entered by the operative or inspector, and then punched manually before the card is read into the computer. If the dual-purpose cards become dirty or damaged during their stay in the factory, they are reproduced prior to computer processing.

Dual-purpose cards are also used in conjunction with pulling files, the item's code number and other pre-determined data, e.g. the price, are in the card when pulled; and fresh data, say the order quantity, is written on the card by the pulling clerk.

Spread cards

Spread cards are devised so as to hold data appertaining to several quite different items spread across the one card. Each item's data is usually self-contained so that in effect a spread card is equivalent to a number of smaller cards joined together. Alternatively a variable amount of data can be punched into the cards within one pack, thus simulating short lengths of paper tape (see below).

The main point about spread cards is that they furnish a means of maximising the rate of computer input. This is because a full card is read into a computer just as quickly as one that is partially empty, it is therefore pragmatic to compress the input data into as few cards as possible.

Paper tape

Data is represented in paper tape in the form of rows of holes punched laterally across the tape, each row being equivalent to one character plus a 'parity bit' that occupies one hole position. The two main kinds of paper tape are 8-track and 7-track, the former contains up to 7 holes for the data and one for the parity bit, the latter has one less hole for the data. The parity bit is a means of checking for errors incurred in reading or transmitting the tape's data, and takes the form of an extra hole or the absence of a hole in order to make the number of holes in each row (frame) odd or even.

Paper tape is punched manually by depressing keys on a punch's keyboard much as with punched cards, the verifying procedure is different however. Here a second reel of tape is punched simultaneously with reading the first reel, any discrepancy between the contents of the first and the keying of the second, results in the punch locking its keyboard until the difference is reconciled.

It is rather unusual for business applications to employ direct-punched paper tape but not so for by-product tape. The latter is created as an automatic by-product from the normal usage of certain kinds of accounting machines, cash registers etc. The paper tape is then available for analysis and checking purposes later, very likely carried out by a computer service bureau (Section 6.4).

Although paper tape is cheaper and less bulky than punched cards [10—see Section 10.2], it is also less easy to deal with manually as regards deciphering its contents, and the off-line sorting and arranging of its data.

Magnetic tape encoders and key stations

It has been realised for many years that the manual punching of cards and paper tape is a slow and cumbersome method of preparing data for input into a computer. Card and paper tape punching and reading speeds are inordinately slow as compared with other means of inputting data, e.g. magnetic tape. During the last few years there has been a gradual increase in the employment of this latter medium as the prime means of entering source data into a computer. Magnetic tape is a plastic material coated with an oxide that is magnetised in a series of spots to represent data, thus resembling a sophisticated version of paper tape. It is mostly half an inch in width and comes in lengths of about 2,400 ft., forming a $10\frac{1}{2}$-inch diameter reel when spooled. Data is recorded in seven or nine channels along the tape including various arrangements of parity bits; the data is very tightly packed, 556 characters per inch being a common density.

Depending on the particular manufacturer, the equipment that is employed for preparing the magnetic tape from source data takes various names such as magnetic tape encoder, data recorder, magnetic data inscriber. Essentially they all consist of a keyboard, an illuminated display, a buffer store and a magnetic tape drive. The buffer store is necessary to balance the high speed at which the device writes data on to the magnetic tape against the relatively low speed of the manual keying. The same unit is used for both recording and verifying, and it also has the ability to search for any particular data record that the operator wishes to inspect.

In operation, the data is keyed-in until the buffer is full, this block of data is then written to magnetic tape which is then automatically backspaced for checking purposes. When verifying, the data on the magnetic tape is read into the buffer store and then compared with the same data keyed in a second time, any disagreement causes the machine to lock until the error is reconciled. The data recorded by individual operators on short lengths of magnetic tape is automatically pooled on to one reel or, alternatively, fed into one multiplexor channel before reaching the computer.

The recording of data directly on to magnetic tape has several advantages; firstly, the elimination of the slow reading of punched cards and paper tape; secondly, the increased speed of keying owing to the improved quietness and smoothness of this operation; thirdly, the avoidance of continual punched card costs since magnetic tape can be used repeatedly.

A further development along these lines is the 'keystation' system. This consists of a number of keyboards, around ten or more, all connected to one small special central processor. The data from the keyboards is automatically pooled and written on to a disk or drum storage device (Section 3.5). After being sorted and edited, the data records are then transferred on to magnetic tape for input to the main computer.

The aforementioned devices are, of course, considerably more expensive

D

than conventional card or paper tape punches but are nevertheless worthy of consideration if large volumes of source data have to be dealt with. As the prejudice against them dies away and as data processing departments become more familiar with their *modus operandi*, their level of employment will undoubtedly rise with a consequent reduction in their costs.

Mark reading (*OMR*)

Mark reading, otherwise known as optical mark recognition (OMR), is the process whereby marks are detected on specially designed documents. The meaning and significance of these marks are determined solely by the computer's program, and thus they can cover an extremely wide range of values and meanings. The actual marks are made by using any black medium such as pencil, ball-point pen or printing. OMR is applicable to applications such as meter reading, time sheets and customer orders.

A meter-reading form has marking spaces for the metered figure and also has pre-printed marks for the account number. These latter marks are printed by the computer along with the customer's name and address (in clear text) prior to sending out the forms to the meter readers. Mark reading is therefore well suited to turn-around documents, i.e. those originated by the computer, then entered with marks manually before being returned to the computer for processing. OMR customer order forms contain a printed list of commodities alongside each of which are spaces for entering marks to represent the order quantity required.

OMR marks can be made by several methods and these may be combined in the one system, the main methods are:

1 By hand using a pencil or ball-point pen.
2 Printed by the computer in the form of hyphens.
3 Pre-printed on the document by a printing firm.
4 Printed from embossed plates along with other information.

Character recognition

The ability of a machine to comprehend handwriting is not yet with us, and is never likely to be in the full sense. Nevertheless the introduction in the mid-1960s of ranges of stylised characters recognisable by computer peripherals was a distinct step in the right direction. The essential problem is this respect was simply that of creating a range of stylised characters absolutely differentiable by a machine and yet fully recognisable by people.

Magnetic Ink Character Recognition (*MICR*)—One approach to the problem is to print the stylised characters in magnetic ink on the relevant documents, and to use a specially designed machine that is capable of reading this printing. The application of this technique is at present limited to bank cheques and luncheon vouchers, and facilitates the sorting and summarising of these documents for accounting purposes. Two distinct print fonts are available, known as E13B and CMC7; the former is employed by British and American banks, the latter by European banks and on luncheon vouchers.

With MICR there are strict limitations on the positioning and amount of the stylised characters, the result of this is that MICR is unlikely to become acceptable as a general accounting media.

Optical Character Recognition (OCR)—This technique involves the optical recognition of printed characters by a machine, it thus has the advantage over MICR in that the characters are less stylised and their printing can be performed by a typewriter, provided it has type heads of a suitable font. There are now many different OCR fonts and character sizes available together with the machines to read them; two main fonts, known as OCR 'A' and OCR 'B' are, however, accepted internationally.

The machines capable of reading OCR fonts are known as document readers and page readers, the former can read one or two lines per document whereas the latter are capable of reading a whole page. Some kinds of reader can accept several fonts and also marks (OMR) and, to a limited extent, hand-printed characters. Tally-rolls are acceptable to certain readers; this capability facilitates the processing of by-product data from accounting machines and cash registers [11—see Chapter 4].

At the present time the main drawback of OCR is the immense cost of the readers; this varies from £20,000 at the lowest up to over ten times this amount for multi-font readers.

3.3 Computer input peripherals

An extremely wide range of peripheral equipment is available nowadays from a considerable number of suppliers. This is in distinct contrast to the situation pertaining in the 1960s when only the computer main-frame manufacturers supplied the peripherals. It is not the intention to attempt herein a description of the full range of devices currently available but merely to outline their categories and capabilities so that the accountant has a reasonably comprehensive notion of the peripheral situation.

Punched card readers

The punched card reader is without doubt the workhorse of data processing, being the most heavily employed computer peripheral in terms of continuous use. It is therefore small wonder that a wide variety of these units is available, covering a broad range of card reading speeds. In general terms the speeds vary from 300 to 1,500 cards per minute and, as explained earlier, the speed is independent of the amount of data in the cards. At these speeds the sensing of the holes in the cards can only be performed photoelectrically, and this being so means that the reading speed is limited purely by the rate at which the cards can be moved physically through the reading device. When one realises that the higher of the card reader speeds entails dealing with a card in only $\frac{1}{25}$ second, it is apparent even to the most non-technical mind that the upper speed limit has virtually been reached. In any event this speed is about as much as the computer operators can handle as regards feeding the card reader manually.

Another way of regarding card reading speed is in terms of the computer input rate in characters per second. A speed of 1,500 cards per minute corresponds to 2,000 characters per second if the cards are full, and lesser rates pro rata if the cards are only partially occupied.

In addition to straightforward card readers, some manufacturers, such as IBM, supply so-called multi-function card machines. These are capable of not only reading punched cards into a computer but can also carry out the functions of the reproducer, collator and sorter (Section 3.1).

Another peripheral device, the reader/punch, combines the capabilities of reading and punching cards, generally the same card is read and then punched with the output results. This restricts card reading to a maximum of about 500 cards per minute since this is the ultimate in card punching speed.

Paper tape readers

Paper tape by its very nature is a much simpler medium than punched cards to read into a computer, its continuous form and straightforward layout facilitate the design of reading equipment. The majority of paper tape readers are equipped to read 5-, 6-, 7- or 8-channel tape at speeds of up to 2,000 characters per second, thus competing closely with the highest input speed of punched cards.

The usual principle of operation is for the paper tape to be fed from a spool, passed through the photoelectric reading head, and then allowed to fall loosely into a bin; it is subsequently re-spooled manually. During the reading of paper tape, parity is checked and any discrepancy automatically stops the paper tape reader.

Document readers

As stated earlier, these devices are generally capable of accepting documents printed in several different OCR fonts, also containing OMR marks and hand-printed characters from a limited set. The output from the document reader is in the form of electrical pulses which may alternatively be passed directly into the computer as with other peripherals or written to magnetic tape for subsequent processing. The rate at which documents are read depends upon their physical dimensions and the amount of OCR printing on them. Before adjudicating the various models, one should be careful to ascertain their precise capabilities in terms of document dimensions, readable lines per document, characters per line, and acceptable OCR fonts.

In general terms, document readers are capable of handling up to 800 documents per minute, corresponding to approximately 1,000 characters per second. Other facilities available on some document readers include the repeated scanning of unrecognised characters, automatic stopping when paper jams occur, mixed document sizes, and the sorting of the documents themselves during the course of passing through the reader.

Tag readers

As the name suggests, a tag is a small card attached to goods or manufactured parts for the purposes of stock and production control. It may be divisible into sections that are detached during the handling of the item concerned. Various methods are available for encoding the tags, including small circular holes, typewritten 'ones', and hand-made marks. A tag reader converts the tags' data on to paper tape or magnetic tape at speeds of up to 500 tags per minute. Each tag holds about 15 digits which is sufficient to contain the item's code number and price.

Badge readers

A badge is an embossed plastic card that is fed into a badge reader by hand in order to transmit the data embossed on it from an outstation to a central receiver. Further data can accompany that from the badge by operating switches manually on the badge reader, and on receipt of this data it is automatically punched into paper tape along with that from the other outstations.

A similar arrangement, termed 'source data automation' employs plastic cards holding either 13 or 27 digits represented by an embossed bar code.

On-line input

All the aforementioned methods of inputting data rely upon the utilisation of a transitional medium between the data source and the computer. On-line input eliminates this by providing for the keying of data directly into the computer via a terminal keyboard. This method is ideal because there is immediate communication with the computer and consequently an immediate response can be received from it. The terminal may also comprise a visual display unit (Section 3.6) and/or a teleprinter, these provide evidence of input and display the computer's reply.

The most common uses of on-line input are for dealing with large volumes of customer orders such as encountered by mail order companies, and for the checking of purchase receipts by supermarkets. Real-time systems (Section

4.4) also employ on-line input, often in conversational mode, enabling the terminal operator to have a psueudo conversation with the computer. Conversational mode is employed at widespread terminals to facilitate airline flight enquiries and seat reservations.

The applications mentioned above all thus gain the distinct advantage of a higher degree of control by the computer over the terminal operators' actions. As an illustration of this, when the operator's intention is ambiguous, the computer suggests alternatives from which a choice must be made. Similarly by carrying out immediate checks on input data, certain errors and omissions are detected by the computer before they damage file data or cause other difficulties to arise.

Real-time data processing is also employed extensively by American banks, and to a lesser extent by British banks, for checking the credit worthiness and updating the accounts of their customers. This is accomplished by transmitting transaction data from terminals sited in the bank's branches to a central computer. A more mundane but equally valuable application of on-line input is for the performing of accounting routines by on-line time-sharing services (Section 6.4).

3.4   Central processors

There is no great value derivable by an accountant or other user from closely studying the electronics of a computer's central processor. The central processor can be regarded as the control point of the computer and, as such, needs to be capable of 'understanding' the program instructions. By this is meant the ability to decode the instructions in core store so as to set-up the appropriate circuits to carry them out, bearing in mind that instructions vary considerably in their complexity—from simple tests to complicated mechanical functions such as printing.

Core store, also known as immediate access memory, holds the program instructions in the form of a magnetic representation of 'ones' and 'noughts', and these are transferred into the computer's decoder in rapid succession during processing. As well as holding the program, the core store can also hold data, and this and the instructions are capable of being changed during the course of a processing run. An intrinsic feature of a fully fledged computer is its ability to modify its own program during the process of obeying it—this characteristic is fundamental to flexible data handling.

Dependent on the particular model of computer, the core store is subdivided into various basic units for the purpose of storing and manipulating instructions and data. The ICL 1900 series, for instance, has a basic unit called a 'word'. This consists of 24 bits (ones or noughts) that can represent either four characters of six bits each drawn from a set of 64 different characters (numerals, letters and symbols), or alternatively, a single number in binary form. The IBM system/370, on the other hand, has a 'byte' as its basic unit. A byte consists of eight bits that can represent either one alphabetic letter, two numerals or part of a binary number. These factors are really only of academic interest to the computer user but are, of course, very relevant as far as the programmer is concerned.

A more significant factor, and particularly so to the programmer, is the amount of core store available in a given computer. The actual amount is really only meaningful in relation to the over-all size and mode of operation of the computer in question. In round figures, however, a computer's core store comprises 20,000 to 3 million bytes or the equivalent thereof. The main point regarding core store is that the greater its amount, the easier it is for the computer to perform its functions rapidly, remembering that a not inconsiderable amount of core is taken by the software (Chapter 4).

· Another factor relevant to a computer's central processor and core store is the speed at which they can between them perform the program. The comparison of one computer with another is not necessarily straightforward in this respect, this is because different computers function internally in diverse ways. Various yardsticks have been adopted in the past such as the time to add together two numbers of a given length or the time to access a unit of data in core store, i.e. the cycle time; but none of these is universally accepted and, in any case, precise comparison is largely valueless. The speeds we are discussing are measured nowadays in nanoseconds (one nanosecond is one thousand millionth of a second), typically a medium-size computer adds together two five-digit numbers in 1,000 nanoseconds, that is one microsecond or a millionth of a second. This time varies roughly ten to one either way from small to very large computers.

Visible record computers and mini-computers

A truly vast range of electronic machines is now on the market, comprising visible record computers, electronic accounting machines, mini-computers and punched card computers. The principal dissimilarity between these and the larger, fully fledged computers is the increased manual involvement needed for their operation; this is especially true for the first three of the above machines. Their speed of operation is geared to that of the keyboard operator since this is the means of data input, nevertheless their internal speed is high enough to avoid impeding the highest rate of input. Apart from this their input/output peripherals and storage devices are fairly comprehensive and include most of those described in this chapter.

The visible record computer earns its name from its ability to read and write on magnetically striped cards, these also hold a visibly printed record of their contents. The cards are updated by being inserted into the machine— either manually or automatically, and their magnetic stripes re-recorded from the transaction data keyed in manually. Each such card holds between a few score and a few hundred digits and so it is ideally suited to a single account.

For small companies with comparatively little data processing, these classes of machines provide considerable calculating power combined with a high degree of flexibility. It is no use pretending however that they can compete with larger computers when called to deal with heavy work loads.

Real-time computers

The hardware of a real-time computer is not fundamentally different from that of an orthodox batch-processing computer—the difference lies in its mode of use (Section 4.4). It is, however, generally true that a real-time system comprises more equipment, including terminals and communication lines. Since the purpose of a real-time system is to provide an immediate response from the computer, a high level of reliability is required otherwise breakdowns would destroy the whole concept of real-time. Consequent upon this requirement, the system's hardware is wholly or partially duplicated, and the hardware units are also inter-connected so as to enhance the over-all reliability.

A real-time computer has to cope with a variety of input messages coming from a large number of terminals via communication lines. To facilitate this problem, a multiplexor or line control unit is used to act as an intermediary between the communication lines and the computer. In this role the line control unit assists the computer by presenting the terminals' messages to it in an assembled and orderly form. Without this assistance the computer would have to cope with a jumble of message fragments as received randomly from the terminals.

Most company accountants are unlikely to come into contact with real-time hardware since their work does not normally have the immediacy associated with such systems. Further explanation is furnished in Section 4.4 however, and this may be of interest to bank and building society accountants.

3.5 Computer storage devices

Core storage has already been referred to in the section on central processors and, as stated, is intended primarily for the accommodation of programs. Unfortunately it is too expensive for holding large volumes of data although ideally it could be used for extensive files. At present, mainly for economic reasons, we must make do with other, less expensive, storage devices. The unfortunate fact of the matter is that these cheaper devices all give slower access to the stored data than does core storage. The reason for this is that they all involve some form of mechanical movement of the various media upon which the data is recorded, whereas core storage does not have this disadvantage.

Magnetic tape

Magnetic tape was the earliest form of magnetic storage detachable from the computer. It was first brought into use with business computers in the late 1950s as a faster alternative to large packs of punched cards. Once the initial problems of manufacturing and processing magnetic tape had been solved, an immense step forward had been taken in the data processing world. Even at that time magnetic tape had a speed of over twenty times that of punched cards as far as the input and sorting of data were concerned. Since then the differential has increased enormously, but to be realistic, it is now invidious to compare them because other media and new methods have interceded.

As mentioned earlier, the material from which magnetic tape is produced is similar to that used in domestic tape recorders, but has to be of a much higher quality in order to provide the extremely accurate recording needed for data as opposed to music and speech. A broad range of read/write speeds are available with the different equipments on the market. The speed at which magnetic tape operates depends upon two factors—the recording density of the data on the tape, and the speed at which the tape physically passes the read/write head. Thus, for instance, a recording density of 800 bytes per inch combined with a movement speed of 75 inches per second give a peak data transfer rate of 60,000 bytes per second. Actual rates vary from a few thousand up to 320,000 bytes per second per tape deck. These rates are, of course, theoretical maxima and under practical conditions they are not always attained; the reason for this is apparent from the description below of the manner in which magnetic tape functions.

For data processing purposes business data is formed into records, e.g. a cash receipt, and each record is designated by a key such as a receipt number. These records are normally held in the sequence of their keys on the magnetic tape, and processed in this manner by being transferred to and from core store. Owing to the limited size of the core store, only a certain number of records can be accommodated therein at any one time. This amount is called a 'data block' and is transferred to and from input/output buffer areas in core store. During the time that the buffers are being loaded and unloaded, the tape must be moving at full speed but owing-to the necessity of reloading the buffer between blocks of data, the tape decelerates to a halt between blocks. This causes short lengths of tape to be unrecorded, i.e. hold no data, and these are known as inter-block gaps.

When reading data into the core store from magnetic tape, the extent to which these inter-block gaps reduce the tape's over-all speed depends mainly upon (a) the size ratio of the block to gap, and (b) whether the block of data in the input buffer can be dealt with before it is necessary to start decelerating the tape. Double buffering is a technique for alleviating these problems but this and many other technical factors relating to the control and handling of magnetic tapes are not of any real relevance to the accountant's needs. Of greater concern is the way in which this medium is employed for accounting purposes.

The principle behind most regular routines involving magnetic tape is to read brought-forward records from one reel and, after updating them, to write the carried-forward records to another reel. Any records not requiring updating are merely copied identically from the one reel to the other. This technique is obligatory from the technical aspect and also secure and convenient from the system aspect. Security is innate because the original brought-forward data remains completely intact on the reel being read and can stay thereon until the carried-forward data is validated later. The brought-forward records can be reprocessed if necessary, together with the updating transactions, but this extra work is not normally required. (See Section 4.6 for further information.)

Magnetic drums

These are capable of providing comparatively rapid access to small files or to application programs awaiting transfer into core store. They are a direct method of accessing data as opposed to the serial mode of magnetic tape, and therefore are much more suited to routines needing access to individual records and to records randomly.

The principle of magnetic drums—the larger of which are called 'file drums', is the recording of data on the magnetised surface of a revolving cylinder. The records comprising the stored data are concatenated on tracks circumscribing the cylinder and each such track has its own read/write head. It is apparent from this that the time taken to gain access to a particular record depends upon its position relative to the track's read/write head at the instant it is called for. The average access time (latency) is the time taken for half a revolution, this figure is taken as a measure of a drum's accessibility—a typical time being 100 milliseconds (one hundredth of a second).

The storage capacities of the different models of magnetic drums vary enormously and, if required, several drums are connected to one central processor. The range of storage capacities available is from 100,000 to 4 million bytes per drum dependent on the particular model, the larger drums having as many as 800 tracks with the corresponding read/write heads.

Magnetic disks

Magnetic disks have the same advantage as magnetic tape in being able to hold a large amount of data, and also that of magnetic drums in providing direct access to the data. In order to hold the much larger number of records, more magnetised surface has to be available than is practicable with drums, and this is achieved by employing the surfaces of a pack of disks. Each disk surface comprises a number of concentric bands of data, and the disks themselves are attached to a rotating shaft so that they all rotate in unison. The outer surfaces of the two endmost disks in a pack are not used for holding data, this means an 11-disk pack actually has 20 recording surfaces.

Magnetic disk units are of two basic kinds—fixed disks, and exchangeable (or removeable) disks. Fixed disks are of larger capacity than exchangeable but, as the name suggests, the disks themselves cannot be detached from the computer—like drums they are a permanent storage media. Exchangeable disk units, on the contrary, use disk packs or cartridges that can be easily loaded on to the unit when the data on them is required. This means that an unlimited amount of files can be held on exchangeable disks, and as files are usually required only one or two at a time, EDUs are a more economic method of storage than are fixed disks. The latter do, however, provide more storage on-line at any one time but need magnetic tape to load and unload them. Apart from these considerations, these two kinds of disk units are essentially the same in their mode of operation.

In order to read and write data, there is normally one read/write head per disk surface, and all the surfaces' heads move in unison so that they are positioned over the equivalent bands at any moment. By positioning the records wanted during one processing run on these equivalent bands, their average access time is minimised because little or no head movement takes place. Such a set of data is known as a 'cylinder' or 'seek area', and there are as many cylinders in a pack as there are bands on a disk surface, e.g. 200. The amount of data transferred at a time is a 'block' or 'bucket', and its size is determined largely by the characteristics of the disk unit; in keeping with magnetic tape blocks, a bucket holds several records.

We again have a wide selection of storage capacities according to the model and the number of packs per unit, the available range is from approximately 1 million to 800 million bytes.

Data cell drives and magnetic card files

A description of computer storage devices is incomplete without a mention of these two devices, although the authors are by no means convinced of their practicability. The two devices are in essence alike in that they employ strips or cards of magnetised plastic upon which data is recorded. In operation, the strips are extracted automatically from a cell or magazine, wrapped around a small revolving cylinder for reading and writing, and then automatically returned to the cell or magazine. The time taken to do all this is from $\frac{1}{3}$ to $\frac{2}{3}$ of a second, and the storage capacity of these devices is of the order of 400 million bytes.

3.6 Computer output peripherals

For all practical intents and purposes the only output peripheral of real interest to the accountant at the present time is the computer's high-speed line printer. This is therefore described below in some detail, and the other output peripherals are then explained more briefly.

High-speed line printers

As seen in Sections 5.1 and 5.3, a knowledge of the capabilities of high-speed line printers enables the prospective computer user to be more sure that he gets the optimum layout for his output documents. In applications involving a large amount of printing, such as the preparation of bills, invoices and statements, the selection of the most suitable printer may well be the dominant factor. Sometimes several printers are used together and it may be necessary to decide between, say, one very fast or two rather slower printers. More often than not however, we are concerned simply with choosing one model from those available on the market.

The actual mechanics of high speed line printing need not concern us here; suffice to say that either a chain or a barrel embossed with characters rotates at high speed, and the characters are printed on continuous stationery by hammers striking this against the embossing through a carbon ribbon. Needless to say, the hammer timing is vitally important, and one can observe the effect of maladjusted timing either as a wavy line of print in the case of barrel printers or as a 'concertinaed' line with chain printers.

Of more concern than the mechanics are the capabilities of printers in terms of the amount of printed output obtainable in a given time, and also their variety of printing. Essentially these factors condense into three main characteristics:

1 The maximum speed of printing measured in lines per minute.
2 The range of characters (the character set) that can be printed at maximum speed.
3 The width of the print bank, i.e. the maximum number of characters that can be printed across one line if all the print positions are used.

The first two of these characteristics are to some extent interrelated because normally the printer can operate at a greater speed if a reduced character set is acceptable. For instance, with a 48-character set, 2,000 lines per minute is possible, but a 38-character set allows an increase to 2,500 lines per minute. The speeds in this example are realistic maxima for the faster printers, others operate at various speeds down to 300 lines per minute. We should also remember that in practice the maximum speeds are not usually sustained for long periods, with the result that the average output is often well below the theoretical maximum. Nevertheless the rate of line printing is very high and cannot be approached by character-at-a-time printers such as teleprinters and typewriters.

One reason for line printers not always attaining their top speed is the need to space or skip between lines of print—this is a characteristic of most business documents. Skipping occurs at 30 to 90 inches per second and is controlled either by the computer program or by a band of paper containing holes and fitted to the printer as required.

The general spacing of computer print is ten characters per inch horizontally and six or eight lines per inch vertically. We can thus calculate the expected rate of output of documents from a print-limited run. If we were printing statements on six-inch deep documents with an average of six transaction lines, three name and address lines, plus a balance, i.e. ten lines altogether, the maximum rate is determined as follows:

10 lines of print at, say, 1,200 lines per minute $= \frac{1}{2}$ sec
5 inches of skipping (6 inches less 10 lines) at 30 inches
    per second $= \frac{1}{6}$ sec
Total time per statement $= \frac{2}{3}$ sec
Output is therefore 5,400 statements per hour.

The third characteristic, the print bank width, dictates the maximum width of printing across the document. In practical terms there is no great limitation since print bank widths are from 96 to 160 print positions, corresponding to documents of about 11 inches to 18 inches in width. A point to remember is that spaces also occupy print positions so that, for example, although a print bank might have 120 print positions, only perhaps half of these show actual printed characters on a given document.

Narrow documents can, of course, be prepared by employing only a portion of the print bank. And it is possible to make best use of a wide printer by printing several narrow documents side-by-side simultaneously.

Visual display units

In view of the as yet limited usage of visual display, an amazingly wide range of equipment is on offer by sundry manufacturers. Similarly, it has caught the imagination of technical authors, with the result that much theorising has surrounded them. Nevertheless, under the right circumstances, visual display provides facilities that cannot be matched by any other peripheral device.

In substance a visual display unit consists of a cathode ray tube and a keyboard together with the associated electronics. The tube is basically the same as in a monochrome television set but is intended for displaying static information rather than moving pictures. For technical applications the visual display takes the form of diagrams that are modifiable by means of a light pen. This technique facilitates the designing of bridges, buildings etc. For business use, rows of figures and descriptions are displayed—not dissimilar from printed output. The main characteristic of displayed output is its rapid formation, it is therefore well suited to situations in which quick inspections of sets of figures are required, at board meetings and other decision-making functions for instance.

Although described here as an output peripheral, the visual display unit can also be employed in effect as an on-line input device (Section 3.3).

The size of the display depends primarily on the tube's diameter, but a large one comprises 50 lines of up to 70 characters each, covering an area twelve inches square. Each character is $\frac{1}{8}$ inch high and the whole display is regenerated at a rate of 40 frames per second so as to give the impression of a steady display. Smaller, less expensive, units are also obtainable, and so is a wide variety of visual display hardware and software.

From the accountant's point of view, the visual display unit can be regarded as either merely an interesting toy or, alternatively, as a vital communicating device with the computer and its files. The choice of attitude depends upon the accountant himself, his need for sophisticated information, and finally the system's ability to provide this. If there is a genuine need for the rapid inspection of accounting figures, this type of hardware is unsurpassed. On the other hand, if it is not utilised to best advantage, visual display is an expensive bauble.

Microfilm equipment

A comparatively recent innovation is the output of computer data on to microfilm via magnetic tape. A microfilm recorder reads the magnetic tape at its characteristic speed and transfers the data to 16-mm roll film or microfiche. Another device, the microfilm viewer or optical image unit, magnifies the film on to a screen 14×11 inches so that it can be read by people. A variety of other equipment, such as processors, duplicators and printers, is also available as part of the microfilm range.

For the storage of historical and archival records of low activity, microfilm is cheap and convenient; for general data processing purposes it has yet to prove its worth.

Chapter 4 **Computer Software**

4.1 What is software?

The word 'software' has been truly coined—if not to say counterfeited into existence. It arises from the desire to differentiate between the computing equipment itself on the one hand, and the means of controlling that equipment on the other. Software has long since become an accepted term in the computer world but nevertheless its precise meaning is still somewhat ambiguous and this situation is unlikely to lessen with future developments in data processing.

In the early days of computers, software consisted merely of straight programs that were fed into the computer and then obeyed immediately by it. This procedure was not regarded in those days as being of sufficient calibre to justify the name 'software' but, as time progressed, various computers began using the same programs or parts of programs (sub-routines). This practice engendered a common computer currency and the need to name it— hence software in contrast to hardware.

Software can nowadays be taken to include application programs, sub-routines, application packages (Chapter 10), operating systems (Section 4.3), compilers (Section 4.2) and, to some extent, d.p. systems and consultancy in general. It is evident from this assortment that software covers a wide range of work and that it is by no means a trivial aspect of computing. In many cases the over-all cost of a d.p. system includes a significant proportion of software costs. Its importance is emphasised by the comparatively recent separation of the computer manufacturers' charges into hardware and software, known by the dreadful word 'unbundling'. Another emphatic pointer to the importance of software is the growth of the software industry, during the latter years of the 1960s several hundred firms came into existence in the UK solely to meet the demand for software of all types. As is usual with mushroom industries, some of the software firms have not survived and many others are of doubtful profitability but, nevertheless, this industry as a whole is likely to expand rather than contract during the next decade. It is confidently forecast that the market potential for software in the UK alone will reach tens of millions of pounds sterling by the late 1970s. This situation of an expanding software industry but containing some doubtful runners means that the software user, and in particular the data processing manager and the accountant, must investigate the alternatives carefully and chose those software houses that appear the most likely to provide continuing service. This latter point is particularly relevant to the use of time-sharing and bureaux services. Whichever firm is selected it must not only be economic in its charges but also permanent in its service.

The main feature of software directly affecting the accountant is the scrutiny and choice of accounting application packages. These are described in Chapter 10, and although such packages have not yet come into extensive use, there is always the possibility that new or existing packages will provide for the accountant's requirements. If this be the case, considerable savings in programming costs and the time taken can result. When investigating these packages it is important to consider their flexibility in relation to possible future requirements as well as their present efficacy. Another characteristic of a package that is obviously consequential is its precise functions. The package user should be absolutely certain what operations the package is performing and what results it provides under all circumstances. It is not unknown for the recipient of a package's output to display ignorance of its real meaning even after avowedly making use of it for several years.

4.2   Programming

In the early years of computers, program writing was regarded as being an esoteric art to be eschewed by ordinary folk. There are still remnants of this idea about, and programmers are sometimes inclined to promote it by wrapping their work in a cloak of technicalities. The man with a problem to be programmed can then be left with the notion that his is the one and only problem that defies simple programming. It is practically axiomatic that a person working at the detailed level of a programmer finds it difficult to truly comprehend the over-all problem. On the other side of the coin we have the person who has attended a brief programming course—usually in a high level programming language, and as a consequence regards programming merely as a trivial and facile exercise. This view is reinforced if that person himself subsequently writes a brief straightforward program, and especially if this is constrained to run on the computer. Neither of these attitudes gives an accurate representation of programming or of the professional programmer. In keeping with most other occupations, programmers vary considerably in the depth of their knowledge and skill, and this is, of course, reflected in their work, status and salaries. Ranging from junior programmers writing small pre-flowcharted program modules up to programming managers and compiler writers who have responsible positions and high levels of skill, the salaries vary in the ratio of three to one. In regard to these points the occupation of programmer is similar to many others including that of accountant in the wider sense.

It is not the intention herein to describe programming in great detail, there are many books and manuals covering the subject in both depth and breadth. It is, however, worthwhile for the accountant to understand the main terminology and what is involved in program writing.

Programming languages

As we have seen, a computer operates by de-coding sets of electronic pulses so as to activate the appropriate circuits and mechanical components of which it is comprised. In order to do this, the computer must have program inserted into it and this is held in such a way that it can be de-coded very rapidly and repeatedly. In the early computers (circa 1950) the programs as written were virtual images of the coded pulses with the result that tremendous amount of human effort was expended in preparing even the simplest of programs. It soon became evident that this volume of work could be reduced to some extent by the use of sub-routines. These are short pieces of program used repeatedly in the one or in several programs, and held in pre-programmed form for quick insertion into complete programs being written. Although this procedure helped, it only scratched the surface of the problem—and indeed could only be expected to so do by its very nature.

The introduction of so-called 'second-generation' computers during the late 1950s brought with it the philosophy of allowing the computer itself to assist with the production of its own program. The concept behind this arrangement is to permit the programmer to write much simpler instructions which are then translated by another program into the more detailed instructions that can be understood by the computer. In the early stages of this development the translation was one-for-one, each of the written instructions being converted into one computer instruction. This technique has developed over the years into what are now termed 'programming languages', and which are capable of converting one written 'statement' into several, and sometimes many, instructions for the computer. Thus although the programmer writes merely a few lines on a programming sheet, the computer receives eventually a large number of instructions to be obeyed in performing its task. The statements written by the programmer are known as the 'source' program, the instructions actually executed by the computer comprise the'object' program. The special program employed to convert the former into the latter is known as an 'assembler' or a 'compiler'. An assembler converts a low-level language, that is one which has roughly a one-for-one statement/instruction relationship with the object program. A compiler converts a high-level language, that is one which produces several instructions from one written statement.

On the face of things one would be inclined to assume that using a high-level language is always the best answer. Unfortunately, as with most things, the benefits have to be weighed against the disadvantages, and in this case the drawback of high-level languages is their inherent inefficiency. This means that a specific job if programmed in two ways—using a high-level language on the one hand and a low-level language on the other, will almost certainly be slower to run on the computer and will occupy more computer storage in the former case than the latter. With jobs that are extensive and carried out frequently—as many are, the computer is then not being used as effectively as possible. This inefficiency normally manifests itself as extra time required to carry out the job on the computer. The associated cost, if recurring, has to be balanced against the once-only savings in programming cost and effort acquired through using a high-level language.

There are nowadays rather fewer languages than at one time because the need to standardise has largely resulted in the disappearance of languages specific to one type of computer only. At present a language must be applicable to a range of computers and preferably to any modern computer regardless of its size, configuration or manufacturer, in other words it must be 'machine-independent'.

COBOL—Typical of the high-level machine-independent languages, COBOL (COmmon Business Oriented Language) was originally specified in 1959 by the US Department of Defense in order that all their computers could be programmed by any programmer. Since 1959 various modifications and improvements have been made, and these are covered by a series of reports specifying the latest characteristics and capabilities of COBOL, the most recent report is COBOL-65.

It must be remembered that although COBOL is now applicable to any computer, this is so only because in each case a compiler has been written to convert the source language (COBOL) into the appropriate object program. In spite of all the extensive planning and compiler-writing behind COBOL, and although it is fairly easy to learn, it is still a language for professional programmers rather than for the man-in-the-street. It is not really a language that can be used occasionally by non-programmers, and regular contact with it is necessary if painstaking re-learning of its peculiarities is to be avoided. Another relevant point about COBOL is that considerable experience in its practical usage is needed to obtain high efficiency from the computer.

Briefly, COBOL consists of four divisions, the first of which informs the computer about the job being programmed, by whom, when and so on; this is the 'Identification' division. Following this is the 'Environment' division, this describes the computer(s) on which the program is to be compiled and run, also specifying the particular peripherals to be used for input, output and storage. The third, 'Data', division specifies in exact detail the contents and layout of the input, output and file data. Each piece of data in the data division is uniquely named and these names are referred to in the environment and 'Procedure' divisions. The latter, as its name suggests, takes the form of a variable number of structured statements telling the computer explicitly what is required of it, in other words the procedure division is the computer's instructions.

COBOL statements are written as English words selected from a restricted range together with data names from the data division. A typical statement might be 'MULTIPLY PRICE BY QUANTITY-A GIVING COST-A'. In this statement 'price', 'quantity-A' and 'cost-A' are data names, the other words are drawn from the COBOL range.

The future of COBOL is somewhat obscure, but as things stand at present, it is by far the most universal business language.

FORTRAN—Another prominent language, which cannot go unmentioned, is FORTRAN (FORmula TRANslator). Again this is a universal high-level machine-independent language but it is generally more suited to mathematical and scientific problems than to business applications. There are, however, certain business problems that are susceptible to solution using FORTRAN, these are usually once-only or annual jobs for which efficiency of running is less important than ease of programming, for example, the annual stock evaluation. FORTRAN is undoubtedly the simplest universal language to learn and to use provided the problem lends itself to being expressed in algebraic terms. The appearance of a FORTRAN program as written differs considerably from COBOL, the above calculation, for instance, could be written 'COST-A = PRICE*QUANTITY-A' or, more probably, merely 'C = P*Q'.

FORTRAN has the advantage of being more suitable for occasional use by amateur programmers, and in this way is employed extensively by scientists, engineers and lecturers. The experienced user can accomplish a surprisingly wide range of work using FORTRAN but usually at the expense of computer efficiency if the work is non-mathematical. This language comes in several versions, one of the latest being FORTRAN IV, and all computers are now capable of compiling it.

ALGOL—This is another universal high-level language, intended for dealing with certain types of mathematics. ALGOL (ALGorithmic Oriented Language) is only likely to be encountered in fields such as operational research, econometrics and technical design.

PL/1—Programming Language/One not only embodies most of the important elements of COBOL, FORTRAN and ALGOL but extends even further by including additional facilities not found in these languages.

Although this comprehensiveness has many advantages and might appear to be the solution to all problems, PL/1 has not yet become the universal language that it was originally intended to be. It is however used extensively by the users of IBM computers, understandably since this company promulgates PL/1.

PLAN—This is the basic programming language of the ICL 1900 series of computers and as such is a low-level language, most PLAN (Programming LAnguage Nineteenhundred) instructions being equivalent to only one object program instruction. Several versions of PLAN are available, related to the amount of core store with which the user's computer is equipped, and having different capabilities to suit the needs of the various sizes of computers in the 1900 series.

PLAN is by no means the easiest of languages to learn—perhaps this is mainly due to its enormous flexibility. It is in practice very much a professional programmer's language. Whereas COBOL and FORTRAN need only one statement to specify the multiplication mentioned above, PLAN requires something like three instructions. It must be remembered however that programs written in PLAN cause the computer to operate more efficiently than do those written in COBOL. Thus for regular and lengthly jobs, the considerable additional programming effort is worthwhile.

BASIC—This language was developed to meet the need for a simple, easily learned language having most of the facilities of COBOL, FORTRAN and ALGOL. In particular, BASIC (Beginners' All-purpose Symbolic Instruction Code) caters for non-computer people such as students wishing to use a computer in their studies. The original concept was that BASIC would be used in a time-sharing environment, for instance to enable students to communicate with a computer via remote terminals. More recent developments enable BASIC to be used on any computer with a FORTRAN IV compiler, thus making it available for conventional systems. BASIC has therefore become a working language for time-sharing systems and also a training medium for general programming. It is not likely however that it will come into general use for business applications.

4.3 Operating systems

An operating system consists of a set of programs held permanently in the computer and designed to organise the flow of work through it. The main aim of an operating system is to optimise work handled by the computer operator(s) by allowing the computer to control the organising of its jobs. The advantages of an operating system become more evident in the context of a large company that has a large computer and which needs to regulate the processing of a large number of small jobs on the computer. Without an operating system human intervention in the operation of the computer can absorb a significant proportion of the computer's working time.

There are, in fact, a wide variety of operating systems, mostly created by the computer manufacturers and therefore geared to the capabilities of their respective machines. Along with other facets of software, operating systems have acquired their own names such as GEORGE, MINIMOP, OS/200, MOD 4 and so on, and the creation of these masterpieces has engendered a small industry within the data processing industry itself. Apart from some of the universities, it is very unusual for a computer user to create his own operating system—there are generally enough problems merely in preparing the application programs.

A criticism aimed at the manufacturers' comprehensive operating systems is that they occupy too much storage, both in the computer's core and its disk storage. This is certainly a valid criticism if the user's jobs are not such as to need many of the operating system's capabilities. It can happen that half a million or more characters of storage are occupied by the operating system, thus necessitating a more expensive computer. If the user can tolerate a lower standard of computer over-all performance, the operating system needed is smaller and money is saved in the reduced amount of core required to hold it.

The capabilities of individual operating systems are not worth discussing here, but the following summary of their general characteristics will give the reader an appreciation of the wide range of activities that they embrace.

1 When presented with a job to be carried out, the operating system transfers the appropriate application program from backing storage into core store in accordance with the job description inserted by the computer operator.

2 A new program requiring compilation results in the relevant compiler being loaded from backing storage, followed by compilation of the program and notification of errors.

3 File storage is controlled so that the user can refer to his files by name, the operating system maintaining an index of user names, file names and file locations for this purpose.

4 Multi-access on-line processing is also managed, and since this mode of processing involves a number of terminals transmitting multifarious data, the facility of multi-programming is required to a significant extent (see below).

5 A wide range of computer configurations from a given series can be used with the one operating system.

6 When the characteristics of the computer's jobs change from time to time, the operating system is modified to suit a particular batch of jobs by means of operating parameters inserted by the computer operator.

7 Temporary failure of a peripheral unit is accommodated by the operating system switching to other units, these are not necessarily of the same type.

Failure of a printer, for instance, is catered for by transferring the output to be printed on to magnetic tape or disk storage pending the printer becoming operational once more.

8 When trouble has occurred owing to machine breakdown, a postmortem analysis of the situation can sometimes be obtained.

9 An accounting and budgeting system is inbuilt enabling the manager to estimate the separate user costs of the computer. Similarly the usage of the computer is logged for all jobs and hence utilisation analyses are provided automatically.

Multiprogramming

The term multiprogramming is rather misleading in that it refers to the way in which a computer operates rather than to the writing of programs. It actually means the carrying out of several independent programs at one and the same time by a computer. Strictly speaking the programs are not executed simultaneously but in fact the central processor alternates between the various programs held permanently in core store or called into store. This switching from one program to another is so rapid and frequent that they are effectively obeyed concurrently. A computer's peripherals, in contrast, can achieve true simultaneity because they have a measure of independence from the central processor. Once their operation is initiated by the processor, their autonomy enables them to continue for some time under the control of their own hardware, thus leaving the processor free to implement the next instructions. Whenever a program is suspended for the want of more input data or the need to output some data, the processor switches to another program and continues obeying its instructions until the peripheral has supplied the need, thereupon switches back to the original program. This kind of procedure results in a more efficient utilisation of the processor, especially if the multiprogrammed jobs are well balanced.

Supervisor programs

A 'supervisor', sometimes known as a 'control' program or 'executive' program, is a special purpose program that can be regarded as being effectively part of a computer's hardware. A particular supervisor is constructed from a number of separate modules assembled together to suit the configuration of the computer with which it is used. The resulting supervisor is held in a protected area of core store so that it cannot be damaged or interfered with by the application programs.

It is apparent from the previous paragraphs that a supervisor has to cope with complicated multiprogramming procedures quite apart from its many other functions. The most complicated and extensive type of supervisor is that associated with real-time data processing. In a case such as this it is necessary for the supervisor to contend with a number of terminals transmitting a large volume of messages, perhaps of different types and with several levels of priority. Added to this, the supervisor controls the inter-action of several processors and large direct access storage devices. This problem becomes particularly acute when breakdowns and faults occur, in that it has to ensure that no file data is accidentally destroyed, nor terminal messages lost or duplicated.

Returning to non real-time systems, the supervisor is primarily concerned with the following functions:

1 The control of multiprogramming, especially as regards the allocation of storage space.
2 The control of peripheral equipment and the transfer of data to and from these devices.
3 The loading of application programs into core store as and when required for running.
4 Communication with the computer operator and the execution of his directives, normally via the computer's console typewriter.
5 The provision of special programming facilities not supplied as part of the computer's hardware functions, e.g. a division routine.

4.4   Real-time and interactive systems

Real-time computer systems cover a very broad range of applications extending well outside business usage alone. These include industrial process and production control, medical information and diagnosis, air and ground traffic control, and further highly sophisticated systems such as automatic radar tracking connected with defence and space programmes. It is unlikely however that anything outside the business aspect of real-time data processing will impinge upon the accountant's responsibilities, and so the description of real-time given here applies only to applications such as airline and other reservation systems, banking, general purpose accounting, and stockbroking information systems.

The characteristic feature of real-time data processing that truly distinguishes it from the more common batch processing system is the immediacy of its response on receipt of a message. The reader should not allow himself become confused between on-line systems and real-time systems. The former concept merely pre-supposes that the input and/or output data are transferred directly between the computer and its data environment, the response of an on-line system need not necessarily be anything like immediate. An instance of this is an on-line production data collection system that simply accepts input from terminals in the factory and utilises it later for payroll and costing purposes. This arrangement, as such, could not be termed real-time but if, on the other hand, the system was designed to provide immediate information resulting in prompt changes to the functioning of the production process as and when necessary, then it would be a real-time system.

Closely allied to real-time is the 'interactive' or 'conversational mode' system, this type of system implies an interchange of messages between the human user and the computer, and so creates the impression of a man/machine 'conversation'. By its nature, conversational mode must be real-time since otherwise the pauses between the conversational messages would be too long for viability. These systems often guide the user into acquiring his desired information or results, and numerous conversational languages have been created to do this, the best of these demanding little or no procedural knowledge on the user's part.

The most well known real-time interactive systems are those employed by the world's airlines for flight seat reservation. In the UK the two major airlines have systems known as BOADICEA and BEACON, respectively; these acronyms have obvious connotations. Such reservation systems have the capability of accepting messages from hundreds of distant terminals and giving replies within a few seconds. BOADICEA, for example, accepts a very large volume of messages from its world-wide terminals via a complex message switching network. This entails that the system must have extensive direct-access files in order to hold an up-to-the-minute picture of the complete seat booking situation. It must also be competent to deal with surges of messages in such a way that none are lost or accidentally duplicated, especially when technical troubles occur.

Another range of real time systems—if somewhat less conversational, are those implemented by some of the savings banks. These have so far become much more prevalent in the USA than in Britain, perhaps mainly due to the larger numbers of provincial banking companies in the USA. Real-time banking means that every bank clerk is able to communicate with the centralised computer-based accounts files via terminals in the bank's branches, all local accounts records are dispensed with. This reduces the amount of work carried out by the counter clerk in relation to each customer and thereby argues a higher level of productivity per clerk. The counter clerk is, in fact, left with very little responsibility except that of keying the transaction data into the terminal and handling the cash involved. The customer can visit any branch of the bank to make withdrawals or deposits, sophisticated security arrangements taking care of attempts at fraud and overdrawing. Real-time has rather less to offer for current account banking and is not so justifiable economically.

During recent years a number of computer service firms have introduced real-time systems in which the user purchases certain terminal equipment and this is connected to a large computer rented on a time-sharing basis. This effectively gives the user a computer's power whenever it is required but without the need to purchase and instal the actual processor. Some of these systems are especially dedicated to accounting work of various types and as such are capable of providing an accountant's precise requirements. One such system comprises terminals each consisting of a visual display unit, a keyboard and a line printer. The mode of operation is for the terminal user to call for the required program, say sales invoicing, whereupon a replica of a blank invoice appears in outline on the VDU screen complete with the pre-printed headings in colours. Working from the customers' order forms, the terminal operator then keys the account number and delivery code, etc., the appropriate invoicee and consignee names and addresses are extracted by the computer from its file and appear on the invoice outline. The codes and quantities of the ordered items are entered next and after each item the computer responds by displaying the appropriate description, quantity, value, tax, discount, etc., all in the appropriate columns of the invoice outline. Upon completion of an invoice and its visual inspection on the VDU screen, the 'complete' button is pressed. The complete invoice is then printed or stored for printing later, the details are posted to the customer's account, the sales analysis and stock ledgers are updated, and the screen is left blank apart from the invoice outline ready for entering the next order.

This procedure is quick, simple and accurate—mistakes being easily corrected prior to printing the invoice. A similar approach applies to other business accounting work such as the preparation of payslips, bank transfers and so on. There is no doubt that for smaller firms with suitable applications these systems have much to offer. The main problem at present is the economic viability of the firms offering such services in view of the high initial capital costs and the, as yet, small demand for real-time accounting.

4.5 Data files (data base)

It is perhaps wiser to use the term 'data files' rather than computer files since, at the risk of appearing pedantic, these do not really have the same meaning. A data file can more assuredly be taken to mean a set of data kept available to provide the information required by the computer user. A computer file is often taken to mean the hardware of the file unit itself.

The purposes of data files can be summarised as:
1 A means of holding large volumes of data in a form suitable for rapid processing and interrogation by the computer so as to create the required output information.
2 A method of obtaining security and compactness for the data and, at the same time, allowing for accessibility and comprehensiveness.

The planning and usage of files has grown over the years into a deep and extensive subject. It is not the intention here to attempt to cover all technical aspects of file logic because this is the province of the systems analyst and programmer rather than that of the accountant. Nonetheless there are many features of file planning that are worth understanding and these are explained in the succeeding pages. In the previous chapter the hardware of data storage devices is described, we are now concerned with the logical application of those technicalities in order to meet the best needs of the computer user.

File records

There is no inherent or rigid structure for computerised records as a whole. The layout, contents and size of each set of records is designed entirely to suit the system and with comparatively little regard for the technicalities of the computer itself. This makes it somewhat difficult to define exactly what is meant by a record except to say that it is a cluster of data labelled for identification purposes, and which generally provides a certain amount of information in itself. The length of a particular type of record is determined solely by the number and size of fields of which it is composed. And although records can be of widely varying length within a file, it is almost always the case that the fields of a given type within a record are of the same length throughout the file.

Certain fields in a record are key fields or 'keys' and as such are the means of identifying and sorting the records. As a broad concept any field can be a key if the computer needs to use it for sorting purposes, it is however mostly the fields holding indicative code numbers that comprise the keys. Other, non-key, fields hold data such as prices, quantities, descriptions and so on; it is therefore the case that fields vary considerably in size, ranging roughly from one to a hundred characters but mostly from five to ten.

The particular ways in which the different fields within a record and also the characters within a field are represented within the computer depend largely upon the model being used (Section 3.4).

The actual number of records comprising a file differs greatly from one file to another and, in fact, tends to change for a particular file from one period of time to another. It is apparent from these remarks that data files are completely flexible as regards their size, content and composition; this is to be expected as they reflect the variations in the environmental data that they represent.

Shown below are examples of records drawn from three data files:

1 FIXED-LENGTH RECORD

	Field	Length
A	Account No.	4 digits fixed
B	Transaction No.	6 digits fixed
C	Date	6 digits fixed
D	Amount	5 digits fixed
		21 digits fixed per record

2   VARIABLE-LENGTH RECORD WITH FIXED FIELDS

	Field	Length	
A	Account No.	4 digits fixed	
B1	Transaction No.	6 digits fixed	
C1	Date	6 digits fixed ⎤	These three fields are repeated as
D1	Amount	5 digits fixed ⎬	often as required to contain
B2	Transaction No.	6 digits fixed ⎦	all the transactions (n).
C2	Date	6 digits fixed	
D2	Amount	5 digits fixed	

$(4 + 17n)$ digits per record

3   VARIABLE-LENGTH RECORDS WITH VARIABLE FIELDS

	Field	Length
A	Account No.	4 digits fixed
B	Name	10 to 30 characters variable
C	Address	20 to 70 characters variable

4 digits + 30 to 100 characters per record

Record (1) consists of four fixed-length fields and therefore is fixed in length itself, (2)'s variability arises from the differing numbers of transactions held in the record, and the variability of (3) is due to two of its fields being variable in themselves. It is plain that record (2) would become fixed-length if only one transaction was included in every record. This would however increase the total amount of data to be held in the file because the account number would have to be repeated for each transaction. Thus if, for example, 100 accounts averaging 10 transactions were involved, record (1) would mean 21,000 digits in the file, record (2) only 17,400 digits. As regards record (3), this could be made fixed-length by making allowance in every record for the longest possible name and address, i.e. 4 digits plus 100 characters. Such an arrangement is however wasteful of storage since large portions would inevitably be left blank.

Variable length records require either an end-of-record marker or a record length field to enable the computer to process them, these are omitted from the above examples for the sake of clarity.

File classifications

Classification according to storage and processing modes—As explained in the previous chapter, the hardware of a file consists basically of either the direct type (disks and drums) or serial type (magnetic tape). Similarly the logical concepts of files allow for various ways of storing and processing the data—in particular, serial, sequential and random. When using magnetic tape only the first two of these are feasible but with direct access devices all three are applicable.

Serial storage—Serial storage means that the records comprising a file are merely stored contiguously with no regard for their keys in relation to their storage locations (addresses). In other words, they are placed side-by-side in storage simply in the order in which they happen to arrive in the computer. Serially stored records must, by their very nature, be accessed and processed serially because there is no practical means of doing otherwise owing to the absence of any relationship between a record's key and its address.

Sequential storage—Sequential storage is where the records are stored in some sequence according to their keys, it is usual for them to be also processed sequentially although this is not always an absolute necessity.

A typical instance of a sequential file is a payroll held in employee number sequence. Because this type of file has a high level of activity each week, it is most likely that the records are processed in this same sequence. If the file medium is magnetic tape the processing must inevitably be in the same sequence as the storage since otherwise the computer would have to hunt up and down the tape to find the records, and although this is possible with certain tapes, it is not a practical position. When the file is stored on a direct access device such as a disk or drum, it is quite viable to process a sequential file in a non-sequential manner provided the number of records requiring processing is low. An example of a low activity situation such as this is when making weekly alterations to the payroll file to cover employees absent through sickness, only a small proportion are ill at any one time and therefore random processing may be suitable.

Random storage—Random storage and processing must not be regarded as implying any haphazardness in the methods employed. To further confuse the issue, the word 'random' has unfortunately become somewhat synonymous with 'direct'—although these two terms have really quite distinct meanings as is seen from Chapter 3. With random storage the records are stored in a file in such a way that there is no evident connection between the keys of adjacent records. Nevertheless the storage location assigned to a given record is determined directly from its key by means of an 'address generation algorithm' (Section 4.6), and this location's address is exactly reproduceable on further occasions. As there is no element of chance in a record's location, random storage differs from serial storage quite distinctly.

The main advantage of random storage is that no sorting is necessary of the transactions to be applied to the file, this is important in the case of real-time systems (Section 4.4) since the pre-sorting of transactions is impossible owing to the wide dispersion of the input localities, and the immediacy of the output required from the system. Another advantage of random storage relates to a file whose contents is continually changing, i.e. a volatile file. Whereas this situation provides difficulties for a sequential file, a random file accepts the new records as a matter of course and merely generates the appropriate addresses from their keys by using its algorithm.

Classification according to file contents—The true meaning of 'file' within the data processing context should be taken as applying to any batch of data records however impermanent. In this sense a data file is rather different from a file used in a manual system where the term normally implies records of a permanent nature. Consequently we can categorise data files according to their general contents and these categories reflect, in essence, the degree of permanency of the data in the files.

Transaction files—These are virtual copies of the source data as read from punched cards, paper tape or other input media such as OCR documents. The records comprising a transaction file are often sorted into various sequences in the course of running the system but the file nevertheless remains essentially the same. The file data is impermanent in that after it has been utilised in providing the required results, for instance to update another file, it is retained only for a short while for security purposes and then dispensed with.

In some systems few or no transaction files are employed, this is the case with real-time, here the immediacy of the processing means that there is no benefit to be gained from creating a transaction file except for security and perhaps analysis purposes.

Another significant characteristic of a transaction file is its size variability between time periods. This is, for instance, true for an expenses file in which the records relating to expense claims vary in number from week to week in an unpredictable way. If a transaction file is held on magnetic tape, this size variability is largely irrelevant but with direct access devices the system designer might have problems in pre-determining the maximum amount of storage needed.

Master files—Master files are a permanent feature of data systems, and form the data-base of the system. There is normally a master file applicable to each and every range of items connected with the system, each range being semi-static as regards its size and contents. This is not to imply that master files are in any way unchangeable—regular amendment and updating are quite usual but the over-all size and basic contents do not normally fluctuate violently. Typical examples of master files used in computer-based accounting are commodity prices, standard costs, customer ledgers, employee day rates.

The processing applied to master files can be regarded as being of three types: amending, updating, referencing.

The amendment of a master file consists of the insertion of new records, the removal of obsolete records, and permanent changes made to continuing records. These events are not expected to occur at regular intervals but as and when necessary on an ad hoc basis. Amending a commodity price file, for instance, occurs whenever new commodities are introduced into or removed from the selling range or when commodities incur price changes.

The updating of a master file is a regular procedure applying to all or at least the majority of records in order to bring them into an up-to-date state. Typically, the preparation of the weekly payroll necessitates updating all records pertaining to individuals in the firm's employ.

Referencing, sometimes called interrogating, a file simply means that the records thereon are examined and data extracted without changing the file records in any way. This process occurs quite frequently during the running of a system as, for example, when names and addresses are extracted from a suppliers' accounts file in order to prepare payment notifications.

4.6 Other aspects of data files

The accountant, as such, does not need to involve himself closely with the more abstruse techniques of file processing since these are very much the province of the systems analyst and are best left to his discretion. A few techniques are, however, worthy of brief explanation, because by being aware of them the accountant can more readily appreciate the work involved in preparing his requirements and in holding the accounting data.

Security

A particularly important aspect of file processing is obviously the need for a high level of security for the file records. This philosophy is applicable to any file but most of all to master records since these are the outcome of many updating and amendment runs. The loss of or damage to an only copy of the master records involves expending considerable effort in reproducing them and, in some circumstances, this is not possible. The cardinal rule is never to put a file at risk by processing it without first making a duplicate copy elsewhere in the computer's storage. This procedure has become a fine art with magnetic tape processing in what is known as the grandfather-father-son technique. As explained earlier, magnetic tape is processed by simultaneously reading from one reel of tape and writing to another. Consequently when updating a master file, the old (brought-forward) data is read from one reel and the new (carried-forward) data is written to another. Because this procedure is carried out regularly, a hierarchy of data exists and this could extend for many generations into the past. In practice, three generations exist at one point of time so that during a weekly updating run the three versions are:

1 A 'son' tape in the course of being created (written) by the computer, i.e. the carried-forward file.

2 A 'father' tape in the course of being read by the computer, i.e. the brought-forward. This was the previous week's son tape.

3 A 'grandfather' tape, which was the previous week's father tape, retained on the shelf away from the computer for security purposes and dispensed with only when the son tape is validated.

The transaction file must be retained from a previous updating run so that in the event of trouble, the master file can be completely re-formed.

With direct access devices a similar technique is possible by reading the brought-forward data from one area of storage and writing the carried-forward data to another. If magnetic tape units are also included in the computer's configuration, the brought-forward data can also be copied (or 'dumped') on to a reel of tape.

Sorting

Sorting is a characteristic feature of the use of magnetic tape and is, in fact, intrinsic to such systems. The main reason for this is because the serial nature of magnetic tape necessitates the continual re-sequencing of the records thereon in order to process them against other files. A case in point is the sorting of factory job ticket records into employee number sequence so as to process them along with wage rates, already held in this sequence, for payroll purposes.

Another reason for sorting magnetic tape records is to put them into the sequence required on an output list or tabulation. A stock file, for instance, may normally be held and updated in component number sequence but requires sorting into bin number sequence in order to produce a suitable stocktaking list. There are numerous other reasons for sorting files and it should be remembered that this can be into the sequence of any field in the records as well as the fields of an indicative nature. Thus, if it is desired to highlight large debts in a debtors accounts file, the sort can well be into reverse sequence of debt amount so as to place the large debts at the top of the list.

Direct access devices are also concerned with sorting but to a lesser extent than with magnetic tape. The chief consideration here is the fairly large amount of storage needed by the computer in carrying out the sorting procedure. Direct access sorting is, however, much quicker than magnetic tape sorting, and is therefore justifiable if storage space permits it.

There are many sorting techniques employed by computers but their details need not concern us here. It is sufficient to say that a computer employs a 'sort generator program' in order to set-up the most suitable method for dealing with a particular sorting problem. The computer's decision as to the best method of sorting is based on a number of parameters specifying details of the data to be sorted and the hardware to be used.

Searching and addressing

When employing magnetic tape as the computer's storage medium we need only consider searching since this is the only means of finding the required records. Magnetic tape, being in sequence, is merely read into the computer's processor a block at a time and each block searched serially for the wanted record. This procedure is straightforward and perfectly satisfactory in the majority of cases; it is, however, rather time consuming and also inefficient if only a small proportion of the file's records is wanted. It is, of course, essential to access the records either serially if they are all to be processed, or otherwise in the same sequence as they lie in the file—it is obviously not a viable proposition to move back and forth along the tape looking for each record.

The term 'addressing' has a definite meaning within data processing, namely, the determination of a precise location in the computer's storage. In absolute terms a computer must be instructed by its program exactly where in its storage to find a required field, record or group of records. In practical terms this problem is alleviated by using various searching and addressing techniques that enable the required data to be found without the programmer necessarily knowing its precise address as such.

Partial indexing—With sequential files held on disk storage a common method is 'partial indexing'. This involves creating an index to contain the highest keys of the records held in each block of disk storage (Section 3.5). To find a record, the index's keys are inspected in turn and the first one higher than the wanted record's key indicates the disk block containing the record. The block is then transferred into core store and searched serially for the record. Partial indexing can cope with both fixed and variable record files, and can also be employed satisfactorily with any range of keys regardless of their format.

Self-addressing—If a range of keys is not too widespread, that is to say almost all the keys are present in the sequence, 'self-addressing' can be employed. This is a very efficient method in that a simple calculation based on the key of the required record leads directly to the address of the wanted record—hence its alternative but equivocal name, 'direct addressing'.

Binary chopping—A technique for greatly contracting the searching of a sequential index is known as 'binary chopping'. This operates on the principle of repeatedly halving the amount of the index remaining unsearched. This is accomplished by comparing the wanted record's key with one of the index keys, starting at the centre of the index. The search then moves up or down the index depending upon the result of the comparison, each move being half the previous move. This technique enables an index of, say, 8,000 keys to be searched with not more than 13 comparisons before finding the wanted key.

Address-generation algorithms—As mentioned earlier a random file generally necessitates the employment of an address-generation algorithm—otherwise known as a 'randomising technique', in order to find a record's location. These algorithms take many forms and essentially are attempts to obtain a uniform spread of records between blocks of storage (buckets). Consider a set of 2,000 records appertaining to, say, motor vehicles whose registration numbers form the keys. If we decide to store these records in 100 buckets, i.e. 20 records per bucket, it is possible and reasonable to utilise the last two numerical digits of the registration numbers as the basis of the bucket addresses. This is because the last two digits are, we hope, uniformly spread between 00 and 99 and therefore cause the records to be assigned uniformly.

In practice sets of code numbers are not so obliging, accordingly it is necessary to employ more complex algorithms in order to reduce the effect of distortion in the code number distribution. The reality of the situation is almost always that the distribution of records between buckets is not uniform, this means that either extra space must be allocated within each bucket to allow for over-assignment or that the overflow of records must be catered for. Overflow is not unique to random files, it can also occur with sequential files owing to the expansion or insertion of records therein. In any event, procedures are available for assessing the amount of overflow to be expected and for dealing with it accordingly.

4.7 Systems languages

The evolvement of the systems analyst into an accepted profession has, until quite recently, been along informal lines and without any formal qualifications being associated with the job. The wide range of backgrounds of practising systems analysts tended to encourage the idea that systems analysis is a creative art not comprehendable to the majority of people. By the late 1960s a reaction against this notion brought about the introduction of a number of 'scientific' methods for systems investigation and design. The general implication being that if the tasks were put on to a scientific basis, less work would be involved and thereby the shortage of systems analysts alleviated. There is obviously some foundation for this concept, and a study of the 'systematic' methods of systems analysis can do no harm. Nevertheless, in spite of considerable advertising, this methodology has not caught on to any extent. The reader can judge for himself from the information below as to why this could be, especially if he replaces systems analysis by his own job and considers the latter against a background of scientific or systematic methods—the weaknesses of such procedures are then likely to be apparent.

One systems language—DATAFLOW, claims to be a technique for increasing the efficiency of systems investigation by relieving the systems analyst of many mundane tasks. The concept is that much of the work of investigating current systems is merely the collecting together of routine facts, and therefore can be assigned to ordinary clerks with a minimum of training. These so-called 'recorders' write down the details of the present system in a special language named DATAWRITE, and this information is vetted subsequently by a computer for feasibility and definitiveness. After this procedure the systems analyst himself enters the scene in order to interrogate the computer and so decide what further investigation is necessary. There is no doubt that the National Computing Centre has put a lot of effort into this system and has produced some sophisticated programs for the automatic checking of data flows. One is left with the impression that the difficulties of using DATAFLOW would generally outweigh its advantages since many systems are simpler than DATAFLOW itself.

A method called BISAD (Business Information Systems Analysis and Design) resolves the complete process through from background analysis to system implementation into seven logical steps. These steps are similar to the steps involved in the conventional methods of investigating and designing data systems. They do, however, regularise the procedure and ensure that no parts of it are omitted unintentionally. A possible danger with this methodology is that the systems work becomes straightjacketed and, as a consequence, the final system is somewhat rigid and unimaginative. BISAD is, however, well organised and comprehensive, and is therefore especially advantageous as a teaching method in the training of systems analysts.

A third systems language—SYSTEMATICS—embraces a range of techniques for designing and describing information systems. The user of SYSTEMATICS is allowed to concentrate on the data system itself without becoming too involved in the computer implementation strategy. Important features of this language are the specification of alternative conditions. The definition of variable qualities of items, and the classification of information items in the system according to their permanence and hierarchy. SYSTEMATICS encourages the employment of decision tables (Section 5.3) as the means of defining data and alternative conditions and operations.

Chapter 5   Design of Data Processing Systems

5.1   The accountant's participation and knowledge

When it is the intention for an accountant himself to undertake the investigation, design and implementation of the d.p. system within the company, then it is obviously necessary for him to become fully familiar with all aspects of systems analysis. Even when the range of work to be computerised is limited, he must still acquire the expertise needed to create an efficient and economical system. This is tantamount to saying that he should become a full-time systems analyst during this period—both physically and psychologically. It is entirely unsatisfactory for an accountant to embark on systems work and, at the same time, continue accepting the responsibilities connected with his duties as an accountant. Fortunately this situation does not often occur, and when it has done in the past, the systems work has generally been restricted to a few isolated and straightforward applications, thus avoiding too much strain on the accountant himself.

The vast majority of circumstances nowadays do not require the accountant to accept this dual responsibility but instead for him to co-operate with the systems analyst in creating the new system. As stated earlier, the accountant has everything to gain and nothing to lose by acquiring an understanding of data processing methodology. In this respect he is in a similar position to certain other senior employees; the contrast lies in the fact that accountants tend to be in the vanguard of new methodology, and also are in an influential position regarding systems changes.

Not only should the accountant know something about data processing techniques as such but, more importantly, use this knowledge to extract every possible advantage from the computer's capabilities. By understanding these capabilities, he can give consideration to methods and potential advantages not previously feasible. An instance of this is the rapid re-calculation of the standard costs of multi-level assemblies and products when material costs change or constituents are altered [12—see Case Study 8]. The computing power nowadays at the accountant's disposal makes possible a more adventurous prospect in accounting without loss of security nor the need for more skilled staff. He is in no way diminishing his responsibilities but is actually gaining the responsibility of utilising the computer to best advantage for his company.

The information about hardware and software in the previous two chapters is ample for the accountant's needs. The particular ways in which he can use this knowledge to assist with systems design are as follows.

Accounting files

What data needs to be held on files for immediate and future use? For what particular purposes are the file contents to be employed? For instance, random interrogation of individual accounts or regular daily updating of the ledgers. To what extent can existing separate files be combined to advantage, alternatively what existing file data is it beneficial to split up into separate files?

Output documentation

A computer's visible output consists for the most part of documents printed by the computer's line printer. This peripheral, as we have seen (Section 3.6), is capable of providing very versatile print layouts. Consequently it is worth taking advantage of this to give each user of the d.p. system, including outside organisations such as customers and suppliers, the most suitable documentation as regards both layout and contents. The layout of the computer's printing often has to be correlated with the design of pre-printed stationery such as invoices etc., and in this case the accountant has the duty of authorising the precise layout and contents of such documents.

Computer operation scheduling

Because essentially the scheduling of computer work is geared to the availability of source data and to the deadlines for output, the accountant can perform an important function by determining these times for his applications. These ought to be genuine times and, in particular the output deadlines should be realistic and not brought forward by an excessive amount in order to allow for possible delays. The authentic deadlines can, if necessary, be emphasised as being vitally important so that the appropriate time allowances can be made for these when the system is being designed.

Control totals

The preparation of control totals by a computer is normally simple and effortless, the problem is more likely to be the manual one of preparing the pre-totals against which to balance the computer's figures. In really knowing the significance of a particular control total, the manual effort worth expending can be decided upon.

Checking procedures

The user of the various data knows through experience the limits applicable to each lot, and advantage is taken of this when designing the feasibility checks to be applied to source data and to output results. The expected range of invoice totals can, for instance, be utilised by the computer in checking each invoice it prepares so that totals outside this range are rejected. This simple check obviates the ludicrous errors that give the recipients of computer output so much annoyance or amusement. Checks of this nature also are useful for other purposes, such as the avoidance of demands for immediate payment of very small bills, the billing routine can be arranged to postpone demand for payment until the next bill.

Standardisation

This concept applies to a wide and diverse range of data. Whereas with manual systems the need for and advantages of standardisation are not always obvious, when employing a computer it is both beneficial and essential to standardise the items concerned. Examples of this are:

1 The layouts of names and addresses including standardised abbreviations, correct county names and abbreviations, and the inclusion of postal codes.
2 Twenty-four-hour clock system—this reduces the possibility of time errors in data but may introduce complications in other regards.
3 Consistent formats for dates, these are preferably all numeric, and alphabetic names and reversed day and month positions should be avoided.
4 Descriptions of limited length with standard abbreviations and logical format, e.g.
   SHIRT NYLON   36 CM
   SOCKS WOOL   SIZE 8
5 Measurements—all decimal or all fractional within a given set, remembering the advent of full metrication and its implications.

Code numbering

The salient point to bear in mind regarding code numbers in data processing is that they are used both by the computer and by personnel in the company. The design of code numbers must therefore be done with this in mind, and with the human users' needs taking precedence over the computer aspect if any conflict arises in this respect. Another factor to be given consideration is the future requirements of each range of code numbers, these depend on the expansion and diversification of the company.

5.2 Classification and coding

In the majority of cases the ranges of items involved in company procedures have been in existence for a considerable time and consequently are covered by well-established sets of code numbers. These code numbers are likely to have been created originally in accordance with a logical pattern and might perhaps have remained so, but in many cases the logic has been distorted by a welter of amendments and insertions made since it was originally set up. Before committing an existing coding scheme to computer practice, it is advisable to examine it carefully for flaws, errors and imperfections. It might well be that all it needs is 'tuning up' before being utilised on the computer, on the other hand it may be so eroded that it must be abandoned and replaced by a more efficient one.

If a new coding scheme is needed for a given range, great care should be exercised in designing and introducing it. The implications of a change of this nature are more wide reaching than is at first sight realised, consequently the accountant or other user of the d.p. system must resist pressure from the computer department to change a good set of code numbers merely to facilitate programming. If a change is made purely for the benefit of the computer, tangible evidence should be available to justify it. In contrast to this, no user is justified in sticking rigidly to an outworn coding scheme which does not really cope even with the existing arrangements or which is liable to incur many errors if duplicated in the new system.

It is sometimes the situation that no code numbers are in existence for a range of items. Where this is so, the items are usually being dealt with by a completely manual system. Such a range is generally fairly limited and operates satisfactorily owing to the staff's long-standing familiarity with the items concerned. With the present state of the data processing art it is highly unlikely that data appertaining to uncoded items could be processed successfully by a computer. As is generally recognised, descriptive identifiers lack the precision and uniqueness needed to provide absolute accuracy of identification.

It might therefore fall the lot of the accountant and systems analyst to create and introduce new ranges of code numbers. In the most straightforward of cases this can be accomplished simply by allocating and issuing a set of sequential numbers—one per item. Where the range of items is strictly limited and the codes are to be used purely for computer purposes, this method is satisfactory. However it is often advantageous to be able to extract some meaning from a code number quite apart from its function as an identifier. In general this ability is more associated with manual usage of the codes than for computer purposes since a computer can store the item's meaningful data in its files and merely employ the code to look this up. There are occasions however when it is helpful to derive meaning directly from the code without having to look it up in computer files.

In order to inject useful information into a set of code numbers it is necessary to study carefully the characteristics of the set of items to be coded and hence decide which method of classification to adopt. Whichever is chosen it must satisfy the following conditions.

1 All existing items in the set must be catered for and, as far as is foreseeable, all future items likely to be incorporated.
2 The logic should be readily understood so that the meanings of existing codes are apparent and so that new items are easily classified.
3 The meanings inserted into the codes by the classification scheme should not be more specific than needed for the uses to be made of the codes. Over-comprehensive classification creates long unwieldly code numbers.
4 Changing circumstances must not cause the classifications to be invalidated. With most items it is impossible to prevent a small degree of invalidation but this should be minimal and easily corrected by re-classifying and re-coding the items concerned without disrupting the system.

Hierarchical classification

This method of classification is typified by the Universal Decimal Classification (Dewey-decimal) system, as employed by most libraries. The basic idea behind hierarchical classification is that items are grouped according to their most significant characteristic, the groups are then sub-divided according to another characteristic dependent upon the first, and so on. Theoretically there is no limit to the amount of this sub-grouping but in practice it is limited by considerations of length and complexity. When utilising hierarchical classification for codes to be stored in computer files, there are obviously limitations imposed by the restricted amount of file storage available.

A cardinal feature of hierarchical classification is that the value of any position in the coded classification is meaningful only in relation to the values of the positions preceding it in the code. This characteristic is apparent in the example shown in Fig. 5.1 and from which it can readily be ascertained that, for instance;

Agency customers abroad are classified 122.
Private individuals in the UK are classified 113.
Overseas suppliers are classified 222.
Group concessionary suppliers are classified 211.

In the example illustrated, even if all existent combinations of accounts characteristics are included, only three digits suffice to classify them completely.

Faceted classification

This system, also known as significance coding, allocates a digit position to each characteristic involved in the classification. Thus the meaning of every digit is discernible directly from its value and position without referring to other digits. A disadvantage as compared with hierarchical classification

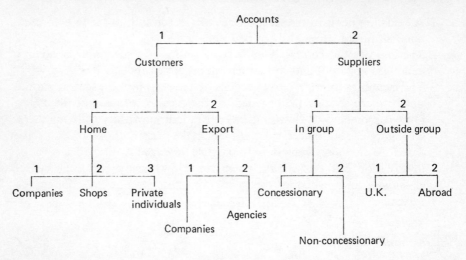

NOTES.
Group suppliers include U.K. only
No exports to shops and private individuals.
No concessions from suppliers outside group.

FIG. 5.1   Hierarchical classification

arises from the fact that more digits are necessary since all possibilities are covered, some of which may actually be irrelevant. Shown below is a faceted classification applicable to the range of accounts used in Fig. 5.1.

1st digit
 1 = customer
 2 = supplier

2nd digit
  0 = irrelevant
  1 = home or UK
  2 = export or abroad

3rd digit
  0 = irrelevant
  1 = company
  2 = shop
  3 = agency
  4 = private individual

4th digit
0 = irrelevant
1 = inside the group
2 = outside the group
5th digit
0 = irrelevant
1 = concessionary
2 = non-concessionary

Using the same examples as before, we obtain the following faceted classifications:

Agency customers abroad	12300
Private individual UK customers	11400
Overseas suppliers	22020
Group concessionary suppliers	20011

It will be noted that in this example the second digit is utilised for both home/export and UK/abroad, since these have substantially the same meanings respectively, it is thus possible to save a digit in the classification.

Allocation of code numbers

The two classification methods described above do not in themselves identify every different individual item within a range. It is necessary to append a few serial digits to the coded classification to provide a unique identification. For instance, if the firm whose accounts are classified as above dealt with 57 agency customers, each of these could be uniquely identified by appending two digits from 00 to 56. This would give a range of code numbers from 12200 to 12256 when employing hierarchical classification, and from 1230000 to 1230056 with faceted classification. In some circumstances classification is unnecessary and therefore code numbers can be allocated in a more straightforward manner, in other cases the allocation is based upon some combination of the various methods of classification and coding. Whatever pertains, the result has to satisfy certain advantages and characteristics as follows.

1 INDIVIDUALITY—the code must identify the corresponding item with absolute precision and each item must have a single unique code number.

2 SPACE—a code number is much shorter than the equivalent description. Whereas a 3-digit code number uniquely identifies 1000 different items, an alphabetic description of eight letters is needed to achieve the same. This represents in computer terms a ratio in storage space of 1 : 5, respectively, and in human terms 1 : 3 in writing or keying.

3 CONVENIENCE—the formats of code numbers should facilitate their use both by people and by computers. This implies a short simple code composed of numeric digits and/or upper case letters only; symbols, such as hyphens, dots, obliques etc. are best avoided.

4 CONSISTENCY—the layouts of all code numbers appertaining to a specific range of items should be compatible, i.e. letters and numerals in consistent positions and all code numbers of the same length. Between different ranges it is convenient to have different formats or lengths in order to facilitate recognition. For example, account numbers could be of five digits (10000 to 99999), whereas purchase order numbers would be four digits (1000 to 9999). An alternative means of recognition is to place a consistent numeral or letter at the front of each code number in a set.

5 EXPANSIBILITY—whatever format is adopted ought to be capable of accepting an expansion of the range without becoming inconsistent. With most sets of items this imposes no undue difficulty since expansion is fairly predictable and, in any event, ample allowance can be made by adopting longer code numbers in the first instance. An example of poor expansibility is vehicle registration numbers, owing to a failure to predict expansion and to the pointless method of allocation, there are now more than a dozen different layouts.

Coding systems

Block codes—With this arrangement a block of code numbers is assigned to a general class or group of items, no detailed significance being attributable to the individual numbers. In allocating part numbers, for instance, bought-out components are numbered 1000 to 4500, made-in components 4501 to 8300 and raw materials 8301 to 8900. Provided the blocks are sufficiently large to accommodate expansion, block coding has the virtues of simplicity and brevity, the meanings and recognition of code numbers are not obvious however.

Interpretive codes—Here the actual numerals in the code number denote a value of some kind and, assuming we remember how to interpret them, a partial specification of an item can be derived from its code. This method is particularly advantageous for a range of similar items such as electronic components or formed metals.

A range of resistors could be coded interpretively in the form such as R2473, in which R means resistor; 2 indicates its wattage in quarter watts, i.e. $2 \times \frac{1}{4} = \frac{1}{2}$ watt; 47 is the first two numerals of its resistance and 3 means that three noughts follow, i.e. 47,000 ohms.

A set of formed metal materials might be coded so as to specify their cross-section dimensions, e.g. SB4315 means steel bar 4·3 cm $\times$ 1·5 cm.

The Brisch system of coding is a refinement of interpretive coding.

Mnemonic codes—Where the codes have to be remembered by people, it is worth considering mnemonic coding. One method is to employ certain letters from the item's description as its code or part of same, e.g. RV = rivet, BL = bolt. By including several letters it is sometimes possible to provide a unique code for each item from a limited and pre-described range.

Another method of employing mnemonics is merely to assign short code 'names' to items without attempting to convey any meaning within the 'name' itself nor to connect it with the item's real description. Code names such as these are applied to many proprietary articles, some even conveying a nebulous meaning, although we tend not to think of them as being codes. For computer purposes these code names are satisfactory provided they are all of a fixed length so that storage is facilitated. A difficulty may arise if the range extends considerably, simply because sufficient names might not then be available.

5.3   Aspects of systems design

It is worth emphasising at this point that a computer system is a means to an end and not the end in itself. When the systems analyst reaches the stage when he feels ready to commence designing a new system, it is worth reflecting on the objectives stated in the assignment brief. These may have become somewhat blurred in his mind during the course of investigating the existing system. Nevertheless, provided no factors have arisen in the meantime to change the situation, these objectives are still the target and must be aimed for. The creation of a d.p. system and a computer department are not in themselves the final targets; they are, of course, merely services to help the company in achieving its real objectives. To the born-and-bred computer man the difference between these attainments may appear academic but certainly not to management if they fail to acquire any real advantages as a result of investing large sums in computer systems.

When considering the alternative system approaches that could be adopted, the systems designer is well advised to keep certain aspects at the forefront of his mind—these are the COST, PRACTICALITY, EFFICIENCY and FLEXIBILITY of the proposed system. Although it is not possible to weight these aspects for all situations, it is usually possible to do so for a given situation and, of course, this weighting of the four aspects is a fundamental part of systems design. They should be borne in mind constantly both by the systems analyst and the prospective user of the new system, and be given relative priorities by taking everyone's point of view into consideration. Thus, although a procedure may be both inexpensive and efficient when being carried out on the computer, it may at the same time, be impractical and inflexible from the user's viewpoint. The accountant, as a prospective user, must not allow himself to be hamstrung by a rigid and over-exacting system from the manual aspect. It has been and is always likely to be the exceptions that prove the system, the system must therefore be flexible enough to assimilate both existing and future exceptions without undue perturbance.

The above four aspects cannot be regarded as distinct features of systems design, they are closely inter-related and so a change to any one of them is likely to affect all the others to various extents. The import given to each aspect in a particular system relates to the conditions, problems and objectives of the respective company.

Computer routines and processing runs

Each application that is to be computerised almost certainly consists of a number of routines. It is likely that these routines will remain substantially similar in purpose after computerisation as when performed by the previous method. A data processing routine is a piece of computer work that achieves results usable outside the d.p. system. An application is made up of a number of routines which, in turn, consist of several processing runs, as shown in the figures in Chapter 7. The actual numbers of routines and runs forming an application differ considerably depending upon the type of computer, the system adopted, and the nature of the application. A typical data processing application is sales accounting consisting of three main routines—invoicing, ledgers, sales analysis. The invoicing routine might, in turn, comprise several processing runs such as order acceptance, pricing, and sales invoice printing. The nature of computer-based data processing is such that the routines are interconnected with one another through the use of computer files, and the runs are interconnected both through the files and the input/output media.

In the simplest arrangement a processing run is controlled by one computer program and is performed from start to finish without interruption except for control and security purposes. When implemented on a larger computer however, it is the operating system and the supervisor program (Section 4.3) that dictate the precise minute-by-minute scheduling of these activities. As we have already seen, these facilities do not affect the designing of systems to any great extent and so the designer need not concern himself overmuch with such niceties. It is, however, important that the systems analyst gives careful thought to the composition of processing runs, and any doubts about the intended capability of a run must be dispelled before building it into the system. If necessary the systems analyst discusses these factors with an experienced programmer and, in an extreme case, it may be advisable to write the program and to test run it in order to verify its capabilities.

The particular elements of a processing run which must be taken into consideration are:

1 The approximate amount of core store needed to hold the program's instructions. With a large computer the amount of core is unlikely to be exceeded, and if it operates in multi-programming mode the core is allocated dynamically as and when required by the program. A smaller computer, such as a visible record or mini-computer, may have severe restrictions in this respect however. It is these latter cases that are the more likely to concern the accountant, particularly if he becomes involved in the decision as to which computer to purchase. The salient point at issue is the amount of core storage that is available for holding both data and the program at the one time. If insufficient is available in this way then extra time is taken in transferring program segments and data to and from backing storage.

2 The availability of peripheral units, especially magnetic tape units and line printers. The designer must clearly not exceed the numbers of these peripherals available on the computer. Generally speaking, a computer run utilises only the one printer since the printed output is of only one layout at a time, e.g. payslips, invoices, statements, etc.

3 The amount of disk file data needed by the run, bearing in mind that this is made available either by loading exchangeable disks on to the units or by transferring data from magnetic tape to fixed disks. In any case the amount of disk storage must be sufficient to accommodate all the file data needed during the run.

4 The sequence of the file records as compared with the sequence of the input data or output results. As explained in Chapter 4, the records comprising files can be organised in a variety of ways both as regards their sequence and accessibility. The particular arrangement of a file may well be decided by the needs of the longest run using the file and so the run in question has limited possibilities in this respect.

5 A degree of flexibility must be built into the structure of the run's program. This means that it can cope with any reasonably foreseeable increases or changes in the items dealt with by the run. Of particular importance in this respect are tables of figures, either pre-stored or created during the run.

6 The need to detect and deal with errors and exceptions. The extent to which this is needful depends largely upon the run's position within the over-all system, those runs closer to the input of source data are more implicated in error detection. In most cases it is satisfactory for the run merely to indicate the error or exception condition and to continue processing the other data. In catering for errors and exceptions it is quite in order for them to be handled manually provided the procedure is properly linked to the d.p. system and, as far as possible, checked by it.

7 The control and audit features to be incorporated into the run (Chapter 9).

The above seven points and their inter-relationship form the corner stones between which the systems analyst designs a processing run. In the normal course of events the accountant need not concern himself with the detail but his general awareness of their features enables him to envisage the inherent problems arising therefrom.

Flow charts

A variety of flow charts are constructed for a d.p. system, differing primarily in their level of detail and comprehensiveness in relation to the total system. At the highest level we have an application flow chart showing the inter-connection of the applications forming the total integrated system (Section 5.4). This flow chart is in block diagram form to illustrate the dependancy of one application upon another but apart from this function it does not provide a great deal of information.

At lower levels it is convenient to segregate flow charts into three categories and although this categorisation is not completely standard throughout the data processing world, the purposes of the flow charts are readily apparent from the descriptions and figures that follow.

System flow chart—As can be seen from Fig. 5.2, the system flow chart illustrates the inter-linking of the routines comprising the total system and shows the flow of data both internally and external to the company. The system flow chart acts as a skeleton upon which further detailed flow charts can be based.

Routine flow chart—This flow chart (Fig. 5.3) is more closely related to the computer methodology and shows the processing runs, files and input/output media within a routine in symbolic form. The symbols used are standard throughout the data processing industry; the principal ones are explained in Fig. 5.4 (British Standard 4058, BSI). These symbols are intended to convey the logical concepts of the system rather than merely illustrating the hardware devices being utilised but in some cases these aspects tend to be synonymous. The lines joining the symbols indicate the flow of data and, strictly speaking, they should always connect with a computer processing run or sorting run. It is helpful to insert a reference number within each symbol so as to cross-reference it to other flow charts and documentation.

The systems analyst is responsible for preparing this flow chart and also those of a higher level.

Program flow chart—This is also known as a 'run' or 'programming' flow chart and as a rule is prepared by the programmer who will also write the

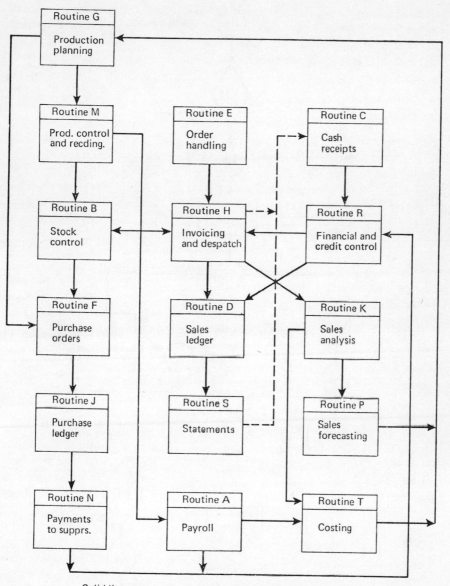

Solid lines represent movement of data between routines, broken
lines represent data movement via outside agencies

FIG. 5.2 System flow chart

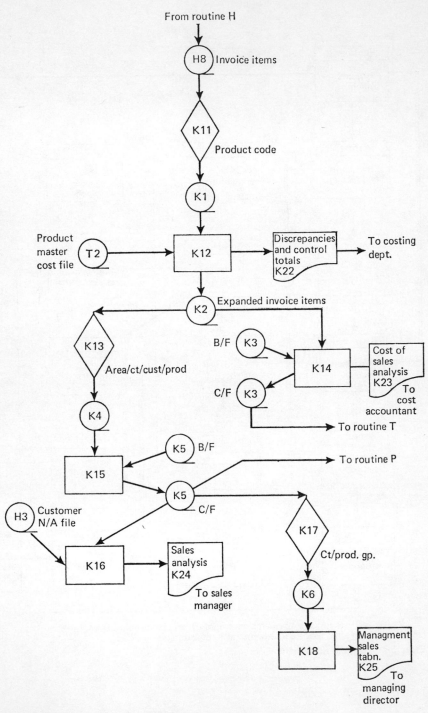

FIG. 5.3   Flow chart of routine K

COMPUTER PROCESSING RUN
A single run, cross-referenced to its specification.

COMPUTER SORTING RUN
The unsorted tape is shown entering the symbol, the
sorted tape leaving it, it is not necessary to show work
tapes

PUNCHED CARDS
Input or output of files or batches of cards of any type.

PAPER TAPE

MAGNETIC TAPE
This symbol may represent a file, deck or reel, and
must be interpreted according to circumstances.

DIRECT ACCESS DEVICE
Represents a file rather than the device itself,
may be sub-divided to represent several files.

MAGNETIC DRUM
Used as for direct access device.

DOCUMENT
Represents (a) source document for punching,
(b) printed output from computer, (c) input document (OCR/MICR)
The associated symbols will make its meaning apparent.

OTHER OPERATION
Any operation not covered by above — especially manual
operations such as punching.

FIG. 5.4   Flow chart symbols

actual program. It is literally his guide to writing the computer's instructions in the form of a list of statements as explained in Section 4.1. The depth of detail and the precise layout of program flow charts vary considerably between different programmers and between the diverse jobs programmed. Nevertheless the primary intention is always to cover every possible path that the computer program can take and in so doing remove any possibility of ambiguity, error or omission. The flow chart should be suitably annotated in order to relate it to the written program statements. Within a data processing department it is beneficial to maintain standards for program flow charting and thereby facilitate programmers understanding each others work, this in turn facilitates subsequent amending of programs when circumstances make this unavoidable.

Processing run specification

As we have seen, a routine is composed of a number of processing runs each of which has a program associated with it, and the programs are written by following the logical steps shown in the program flow chart. Before this flow chart can be prepared however it is necessary for the systems analyst to provide a detailed specification of what the run is intended to do. In addition to this, the systems analyst should discuss the specification with the programmer with the object of removing misunderstandings, and also with the same object in view keep in touch with the programmer during the writing of the program.

The principal features of a processing run specification consist of the following items of information:

1 The exact contents and layouts of input data in the various media such as punched cards, paper tape, OCR documents, etc. Although the actual layouts are not of great concern to the accountant, the contents are, and so he has considerable interest in ensuring that they are complete and correct for his data.

2 The volume and sequence of input data of each type.

3 The checks to be applied to input data and at various stages of processing in order to detect possible errors.

4 The processing steps, i.e. the calculations and comparisons etc. to be carried out by the run. These are very much the user's concern in that they are essentially the means of producing his requirements.

5 Totals, including control totals, to be accumulated during the run.

6 File contents and layouts both of new files created (if any) and of existing files referred to.

7 Output contents and layouts—these details apply particularly to printed output on pre-printed stationery. Print layout charts, supplied by the manufacturer, facilitate the design of printed output and there is no reason

why the accountant should not use these to design his own output documentation.

Decision tables

The more involved and intricate parts of a processing run—and of other procedures, are sometimes difficult to describe in ordinary English without some degree of ambiguity intruding. It is then usual for the systems analyst to prepare a simplified version of the program flow chart in order to explain the requirements with complete clarity. The programmer will in all probability re-draw this chart before attempting to program from it but this is of no concern so long as it has enabled him to understand exactly what is needed.

When the problem is mainly associated with an abundance of alternative instruction paths within the program, a flow chart can become complicated and unwieldly, a decision table is then likely to be the more suitable method for defining the requirements of the program. Similarly a decision table is valuable as the means of connecting multiple conditions to the corresponding actions to be carried out. For instance, to convey the details of the discount scheme explained in the narrative below, the decision table shown in Fig. 5.5 could well be employed.

'Customers consist of three types—large companies, small companies and private individuals. They are allowed discounts based on the values of their orders as follows.

Long-standing company customers get 25 per cent for orders of £500 or

Condition stub — Rule Nos. — Condition entries

	1	2	3	4	5	6	7	8	9	10
Large company?	–	–	–	–	–	–	Y	Y	–	–
Small company?	–	–	–	–	–	–	–	–	Y	Y
Private individual?	N	N	N	Y	Y	Y	–	–	–	–
Long-standing customer?	Y	Y	Y	–	–	–	N	N	N	N
Order £500 or above?	Y	–	N	Y	–	N	Y	N	Y	N
Order £50 to £499.99?	–	Y	N	–	Y	N	–	–	–	–
Discount % allowable	25	20	15	10	7½	0	20	5	10	5

Action stub — Action entries

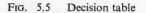

Fig. 5.5   Decision table

over, 20 per cent for orders of less than £500 but of £50 or above, and 15 per cent for smaller orders. The corresponding discounts for private individuals, regardless of standing, are 10 per cent, 7½ per cent and zero. New large company customers get 20 per cent on orders of £500 or over, and 5 per cent on lesser orders. New small company customers get 10 per cent and 5 per cent correspondingly.'

It can be seen from Fig. 5.5 that a decision table comprises four sections— shown separated by double lines. The upper sections specify the conditions applicable to the circumstance, and the lower sections specify the relevant actions to be taken, in this case the discount allowed. In the columns of the 'condition entries' section, 'Y' means 'yes' and 'N' means 'no' as applied to the corresponding question in the condition stub. All the condition entries in a given column must be valid before the corresponding action applies, dashes indicate irrelevant questions.

It is important that the decision table covers all conditions that can prevail under the practical circumstances, and that there is no ambiguity. There are many different ways of arranging the structure of a given decision table including, for instance, putting more detail into the condition entries and thereby reducing the number of rows in the condition sections [10—see Section 11.1]. In some decision tables, several actions are applicable to each rule, and these are shown as several rows in the action sections. The example in Fig. 5.5 is known as an 'extended condition/limited action' decision table because the conditions are put in the form of questions requiring only 'yes' or 'no' answers and therefore need to appear several times each; in contrast to this, the actions are catered for in only one row each because the action entries are more explicit.

5.4 Integrated data processing

Within the context of business data processing it is better to regard 'integra-tion' as meaning the knitting together of the business applications encom-passed by the system rather than necessarily the inclusion of every possible application within the system. Ideally, if the computer is sufficiently powerful, all the main business applications appertaining to the company are carried out by the computer in an integrated fashion. But even if not all the main appli-cations are computerised we can still legitimately refer to it as an 'IDP' system provided the system is integrated within itself and also is open-ended to allow for the inclusion later of other applications, and the smooth inter-connection with external routines.

Integration does not necessarily mean the use of a large computer, a small machine can be used to run an integrated system provided, of course, that it can handle the amounts of data actually encountered. Nor does integration mean that all applications must be implemented on the computer simul-taneously, they may be transferred as and when convenient but at each stage allowance is made for connecting the stages to follow it. The implementation of isolated applications without regard for the others will undoubtedly cause interfacing problems later.

What are the basic principles of IDP?

Data-base—If the d.p. system is based upon a comprehensive set of computer files in which no records are omitted or duplicated, a good start has been made towards successful IDP. The duplication of data is best avoided, especially in master files, since this can lead to discrepancies after amendments to the files have been made. Whenever possible within the bounds of practicality, all the data appertaining to one item should lie in one record. The one product file, for instance, could hold the data needed for routines such as sales invoicing, sales analysis, production planning, and so on.

Since we are endeavouring to cater for all routines—both present and future, by using the same data-base, this entails giving careful thought to the fields to be incorporated in the file records, both for regular processing and interrogation purposes. It is pragmatic to include from the start any fields that can be visualised as being required later provided these do not occupy excessive storage space in the meantime.

Source data—This enters an IDP system once only and thereafter is processed along with other data in order to produce the required output results. It is very inefficient to input any significant amount of source data more than once because this procedure occupies a relatively large amount of computer time. Typically, the data from a production job ticket should enter the system once only and then be processed as often as necessary to provide information for job costing, payroll, work-in-progress control and so on. It is often the case that the source data is written to magnetic tape and this is read during the routines that need it. Since magnetic tape can be read very much faster than source data media, this principle is good data processing practice.

Common coding—Because integration entails the connecting together of the various routines and applications through their common data-base, it is important that the identical code number is used by all routines for a given item. In cases where practical considerations prevent this, the system must be capable of accepting any one of the alternative code numbers as the key to the identity of the relevant item [10—see Section 7.5].

If a changeover from one set of code numbers to another is made, care must be taken to ensure that the d.p. system is capable of accepting either of the code numbers applicable to an item for some considerable time after the changeover date.

Flexibility—An IDP system must not only be capable of expansion in terms of the data volumes but should also be capable of catering for unforeseen eventualities as far as is reasonably possible. This need for pliability is pertinent to any system even if it comprises only an isolated application, it is markedly more true of an integrated system owing to the danger of creating an over-rigid self-contained system that cannot be employed for special purposes without excessive difficulty. An example of this sort of thing is the inaccessibility of file data to anything except the computer. Obviously this is a technical truism but the point being made is that all computer file records should be readily available for manual inspection—perhaps for completely unanticipatable reasons.

It is amazing the extent to which most presently existing d.p. systems cannot cope quickly enough with a change in circumstances. A postal strike, for instance, results in a flood of telephone enquiries to insurance companies from their customers regarding their car insurance cover. The required information is then found to be locked away on a computer file, and therefore completely inaccessible manually, the result of this situation is widespread confusion and doubt as to the customers' legal position from the insurance aspect.

This comes back to the systems analyst and the need for him to envisage all eventualities that are reasonably possible. The accountant's experience of previous unusual circumstances is invaluable in this respect, and it is partly his responsibility to suggest fail-safe methods for his accounting routines in the event of difficulties arising. By so doing he will sleep better in the knowledge that he is master of the over-all situation and that external uncontrollable events will not spell disaster for his computer-based accounting system.

Chapter 6 Implementation of Data Proccessing Systems

6.1 Selection of data processing facilities

After the facts appertaining to the existing system have been gathered together, and the new system has been designed in outline, the systems analyst is in a position to decide in general terms the approximate computer configuration which will be required. This stage involves extensive discussions with the computer manufacturers and service bureau companies. The points under discussion are of a technical nature requiring a level of computer expertise generally possessed only by data processing personnel, neither the accountant nor other management need concern themselves with these discussions except to give advice regarding finance and policy.

There are a number of alternative methods of acquiring computing power apart from actually purchasing or renting an in-house machine. These alternatives are sharing a computer, computer time hire, on-line time sharing, and bureau service. The hardware aspects of these are covered in Chapter 3, so we shall concern ourselves here solely with their relative merits from the user's point of view.

Shared computer

This is a somewhat unusual arrangement in that it involves several firms jointly purchasing or renting a computer and thereafter sharing its usage. The user firms are generally members of a group or trade association and, as such, will probably be carrying out similar work on the computer. The data processing staff may be employed either by the sharing firms as a whole or as separate groups by the individual firms, each of which firm sends along its own staff to operate the computer, and creates its own systems and programs. The former arrangement has obvious administrative advantages because the data processing staff are an entity, acting in effect as a service bureau to the sharing firms.

With computer sharing, care must be taken in planning and scheduling the jobs so as to ensure that all the users obtain their requirements punctually. Accepting this constraint, the result of sharing a larger computer is normally more economic and efficient than each user firm having its own smaller machine. There is no real comparison between the capabilities of a fully-fledged computer with large-scale storage facilities, and the alternative of a number of visible record or minicomputers controlled essentially by hand.

In any event each user company's systems staff or project team should design its system and thereafter keep in close contact with its implementation and running.

Time-hire

At its best this method is effectively the same as sharing a computer, the usage of the computer is generally for a regular pre-booked length of time and the planning of the work is centered around this booking. The efficacy of time hire depends upon a number of factors—the hired computer's configuration, its distance from the user's premises, the degree of certainty of its availability when needed and careful co-ordination by the user of his data preparation and processing.

Hidden costs are apt to appear if events do not proceed according to plan and so it is advisable for the accountant to satisfy himself of the viability of time-hire before committing his work to it. This is particularly important when the time is to be hired from another firm whose computer is not fully utilised, the hired time is then liable to be taken up on occasions by the owner's overloads and re-runs, thus leaving the hirer in difficulties.

On-line time-sharing

This facility entails using a large computer simultaneously with a number of other users—probably doing quite different types of work. The user has a terminal(s) installed in his own premises and this is linked to the computer via data transmission lines. Because of the computer's ability to process a large amount of data from multiple sources concurrently and still respond quickly with its output, the user is not aware of the sharing aspect. An important feature of an on-line time-sharing service that needs to be investigated by the prospective user is its existing and intended loading. The prospective user must assure himself that the computer's loading is not intended to be so high as to cause excessive delays during processing runs. It should also be remembered that an individual company offering on-line time-sharing service might be geared to a certain type of work, and consequently the level of service might not be so high for other types of work.

Although the actual processing costs of this facility are usually quite modest, this might be less true for the data transmission and storage costs involved.

The data transmission cost is generally based on a number of factors such as the distance between the terminal and the computer, the times of day of transmitting, the speed of transmission and of course, the volume of data. With regard to the storage of data, it is obviously uneconomic to pay for the on-line storage of large files if these require to be accessed only infrequently. This situation can come about gradually and remain unnoticed owing to the slow but steady growth of files or their gradual creep into obsolescence.

The various on-line time-sharing service companies offer a wide range of services including application packages and conversational mode working. It is important that the prospective user of this system, and particularly the accountant if regular accounting work is intended to be done, enters into the safest contract for his real needs. The service company must demonstrate its ability to provide an economic and continuing service, because although this system has a big future, several companies offering it have foundered on the way. Nevertheless on-line time-sharing is undoubtedly the answer for large numbers of small firms and also for specialised users in large organisations.

Bureau service

During the latter years of the 1960s a large number of small companies came into being in the service bureau industry, adding their facilities to those of the computer manufacturers' bureaux and a few others which had also been in existence for some considerable time. Some of these small companies mushroomed overnight into what was believed to be a computer Klondyke, other larger companies entered the field from overseas also intending to take part in this mythical gold rush. Understandably a number of American companies based their profit predictions of the UK market on their results in the USA, but owing to the dissimilarities in British businesses and administrations, the potential has proved to be nothing like so great as in America. The outcome of this rapid expansion in the UK service bureau industry is the intensive competition now prevailing, and although ostensibly this should favour the customer, it has resulted in fact in a somewhat confusing plethora of services of various kinds and at various levels. Some such firms offer advisory services —sometimes at a rather superficial level, and then sub-contract any actual data processing work to other bureaux. Other firms provide a complete service from consultancy through systems investigation and programming to actually processing the customer's data.

In the early years of computer bureaux many customers were disenchanted by the service they received. In order to counteract this unhealthy situation, the Computer Services and Bureau Association (COSBA) was founded in Britain in 1968. This organisation now represents the major portion of the UK service bureau industry and guards the interest of bureau users by imposing professional rules of conduct upon its members.

The accountant's depth of interest in the efficiency of the various bureaux clearly depends upon the volume and importance of the work that he has in mind for tendering. Whereas the annual stock evaluation is still quite valid even if it is a few days later in completion, this state of affairs does not apply to the weekly payroll preparation. In other words it is vitally important to assess the capabilities of a bureau before allowing it to undertake any work of great extent or immediacy. This problem is not easily dismissed, there being no direct connection between a bureau's quotation and its efficiency.

What should the accountant therefore do if he requires bureau service?

1 Obtain quotations from several bureaux, all based on identical and precise specifications of the work to be carried out. No points should be left in doubt as regards (a) the exact results required, (b) the source data to be supplied by the customer, and (c) the turn-around timings of the operation. The quotations should be broken down into the separate charges for programming, data preparation, file creation, regular processing, and other work (if any).

2 Ensure that the bureau staff appreciate the amount of preliminary work involved in creating and checking the files, in vetting basic input data, and in handling the output if this is appreciable.

3 Study the contractual agreement proposed by the bureau so that there is no doubt as to who is responsible for what.

4 Check up on the bureau's efficiency, (a) by enquiring about the stand-by arrangements for coping with prolonged computer breakdown and, (b) by investigating the bureau staff's competence in systems design and programming. These points are rather difficult to establish, it is therefore wise to discuss the bureau's efficiency with its existing customers who are having similar work carried out.

5 Ascertain the eventual ownership of the programs and documentation associated with the work in hand. There is always the possibility that the bureau work will later be transferred on to the customer's own computer and so program ownership is consequential.

6 Establish precisely who will be doing each stage of the over-all work. Some consultancy firms offer a 'turnkey' operation—so called because the complete process from investigation of the customer's requirements through to the running of the work is supervised by the consultants on behalf of the customer. This could mean a large amount of sub-contracting with the consequent possibility of later difficulties if things do not go according to plan.

6.2   Testing the data processing system

Prior to testing the d.p. system as an entity, the individual computer programs will have been written and fully tested by their programmers. In practice a few programs of lesser importance may still be outstanding when system testing commences but this is of no great consequence. Like many other complex things, d.p. systems are often reluctant to exhibit their faults until the last possible moment and certainly not before they are assembled together into their entirety. It is, of course, the system designer's responsibility to test the correctness and completeness of the over-all system but nevertheless the prospective user can profitably apply his own checks to the applications in which he has an interest. When all is said and done, it is the users who, even at this stage, still know more about the requirements of the system.

Essentially, the main things the accountant or any other user needs to verify are the accuracy and completeness of his application's output results in relation to the basic input data that he supplies to the system. In addition to this, it is necessary for him to be certain that the data held on his files is being updated and amended correctly by all the computer runs intended to do so. In ascertaining the system's validity, there is a natural temptation to employ real source data that has been used previously, and then to compare the d.p. system's output with that from the former system. Although this method goes some way towards the comprehensive checking that is needed, it is unlikely to be stringent enough. It is often the case that previous real data is rather limited in its extent and depth, and therefore fails to stretch the d.p. system to the degree needed, the result of this is that the more subtle errors go undetected. Consequently the accountant is well advised to prepare his own source data for testing purposes, and from this to calculate the results expected. This is a somewhat tedious chore but is a once-only operation and in the long run is worthwhile because it provides an absolute assurance that all the exact requirements are being catered for.

Idealistically the accountant need only concern himself with 'what goes in and what comes out', the minutiae of the processing runs and programming strategy are not his problem. There are however two problems in this respect; firstly, will the results continue to be correct under all circumstances of input data, secondly, is the system reasonably open-ended? Taking the first of these points, it is an obvious and natural tenet that the input data must be correct if the output results are also to be correct—hence the well-worn adage 'rubbish in, rubbish out'. Although strictly speaking this is not always true under all circumstances, it is near enough so for our purposes here. The second point means that the system should be capable of accepting relatively small extensions and variations without falling apart.

In preparing his test data, the accountant should attempt to cover not only all the basic features of the application or routine but also the exceptions and extremes that could be encountered. The particular factors to be included in the test data are:

1 The extreme values of the input fields and the combinations of field values that give rise to maximum values during and as a result of processing them. For instance, a customer order quantity and the corresponding

selling price of the item concerned should be chosen so as to extend to the maximum selling value that could be expected, as well as covering the separate maxima of these two fields.

2 All possible formats of code numbers and descriptions, especially if these are of several types and are liable to involve slight but significant variations. An instance of this is the usage of hyphens, gaps, dashes, etc., within code numbers, these are often accidentally omitted and although this is usually acceptable in manual systems, it is not so in d.p. systems.

3 Feasibility checks imposed on the input data in terms of its combinatorial values. Whenever a field is found to be in conflict with the value of another field, a suitable error message should be output.

4 The testing of all possible program paths, i.e. all the different circumstances that can arise within a given processing run. This is, of course, very difficult to accomplish in certain cases, but in general it is possible to cover the situation without too much difficulty.

5 The accessing of file records, especially if stored on magnetic disk devices. The accountant must be assured that the correct file records are being used at all times during subsequent processing and that, for example, there is no possibility of one ledger account being updated by another account's transactions. Although theoretically this entails checking every record individually, in practice a reasonable number of spot checks ensures correctness in this respect.

6 Finally, the accountant should be certain that his manually calculated results are themselves correct and in accordance with the intended results from the d.p. system before assuming that the new system is erroneous.

6.3   Changeover to the data processing system

Following several months of system investigation and design, program writing and testing, system appraisal and testing, with probably many after-thoughts and mistakes on the way, comes either the hour of triumph or alternatively the day of reckoning. The actual situation is likely to be less dramatic than these, falling somewhere between, and the extent to which it goes one way or the other depends largely upon the level of the planners' skills, their diligence, and also a certain amount of luck. In any event, there are likely to be considerable headaches before everything becomes entirely satisfactory, so what can be done to minimise these discomforts?

Unfortunately there is no one simple recipe for guaranteeing success in implementing the changeover; remembering the wide ranges of facilities, hardware and applications that could be involved, the reader will appreciate that the problem as a whole is very extensive. Nevertheless certain guide lines are usefully followed and these can be modified to suit a system's individual needs as regards changeover.

It is quite often the case that much of the program testing is carried out on another similar computer prior to the user's own machine being installed, and provided this does not incur too much expense, this is clearly a desirable procedure since it gets the computer into action more quickly once it is installed. The final testing of the over-all system is, however, generally done on the user's own computer before changeover to the new system occurs.

Creating and checking files

The accountant's staff are likely to be implicated in considerable extra work during the changeover period, and this factor must be borne in mind throughout the planning of the changeover. This additional load might be aggravated by last-minute resignations of staff owing to the fear of impending redundancy. The majority of the accounting staff's extra work is associated with the creation of master files and checking the data thereon. The actual physical creation of these files is, of course, the data processing department's responsibility but this operation cannot be done in a void, the file source data must come from the user department.

In the more straightforward cases, a master file is created as a virtual copy of the source data but, more often than not, things are more complex than this. Editing of and alterations to the source data are needed in order to make it suitable for future use in computer files, also it is frequently necessary to combine several lots of data from various sources into one master file. An example of the latter situation is when a master file of sales commodities is created both from a stocklist and a price list, it may well have been the case that these two lots of data had never previously been brought together owing to the original system's different method of operation. This need to combine data brings with it certain problems such as the mismatching of like items due to non-uniform code numbers being employed in the earlier system, this situation is especially likely if a manual system is being transferred. Additionally, items may be missing from some of the source documentation, and this situation was not apparent previously owing to the inactivity of the documents.

There are, fundamentally, two approaches to the problem of creating computer master files. One way is to collate, edit and check manually all the various documents pertaining to a given file, and then to transfer this data to the computer file in one operation. The other approach is to create separate computer files from each set of documents and then, after editing, to collate and check these files using the computer. The decision as to which method to adopt depends primarily on the size of the eventual file. Whereas the former approach is generally satisfactory for a few hundred items, it is unwieldy and very time consuming in cases where many thousands of items are involved. Whichever approach is used, the vital issue is correctness and completeness in the final versions of the files; control totals and complete or partial proof lists play complementary roles in obtaining these objectives.

Another aspect of file creation is its phasing; because a file is generally a dynamic thing, it can truly be regarded as being fully correct only at one point of time. Owing to the considerable time taken to transcribe manually from the basic source documents to the input media (punched cards, etc.), the records are likely to be out-of-date by the time they reach the computer's file. With a large file, the data must be sectionalised and 'frozen' as at a particular point of time, after each section of frozen data has been transferred, the interim transactions and amendments are then applied to it so as to make it absolutely current. The most important matter is to know precisely what has been transferred and updated at every stage so that there is no possibility of duplications or omissions occurring.

Changeover procedures

There are several basic methods that can be employed in changing over to a d.p. system, and these need not necessarily be exclusive alternatives. That is to say, different methods may be employed for the various applications within the one company, moreover different companies may adopt alternative methods for the same application. The plan of campaign is decided well beforehand by agreement among the principal parties concerned but the actual method is largely the decision of the systems analyst after defining the user department's contribution in each case.

Direct changeover—With direct changeover, operations under the old system cease abruptly and the computer immediately takes over. This is a rather drastic procedure and is best avoided unless it is absolutely necessary; there are situations however, such as with a real-time system, where direct changeover is the only practical proposition. Even here the burden of changeover can sometimes be lightened by bringing a group of terminals at a time into operation.

With more conventional accounting systems direct changeover is best arranged to occur at a week-end or holiday period, so causing the least disruption and also allowing extra time for last-minute problems which are bound to crop up. Direct changeover has the advantage of entailing the minimum of extra work in that there is no duplication, but has an enhanced problem in ensuring that the new system is fully correct. This is because there is no absolute comparison with the previous system's results, different source data having been used to obtain these. Another problem occurs if the output from the d.p. system is found to be badly astray, it is then difficult to restore the situation because the original facilities might have completely disappeared in the meantime.

Pilot running—In this case, current data continues to be processed by the original system while, at the same time, earlier data is re-processed by the computer. Thus, provided the two systems are intended to furnish similar results, a basis for comparison exists and thereby facilitates the detection of discrepancies in the d.p. system. The amount of re-processing carried out by the computer during pilot running is normally less than the full volume of a processing cycle and, this being the case, it is important to select a sample of data that is representative in terms of comprehensiveness and exceptions. Several cycles of re-processing, e.g. weekly payroll or monthly accounts statements, should be carried out, and the number of cycles need not necessarily be pre-decided but dependent upon the actual outcome of the pilot runs themselves.

Pilot running is a convenient forerunner to direct changeover and can continue right up to the time of changeover. It is sometimes possible to gradually increase the data volumes employed for pilot running right up to the full amount and then, by doing two lots at the one time, move automatically on to the new system.

Parallel running—This arrangement involves processing the current data by both the old system and the d.p. system, and comparing the resultant outputs. This comparison is perfectly straightforward if the two lots of results are expected to be identical but otherwise an intermediate stage—either manual or computer—is required to provide comparability. All the accumulated totals are compared and also a sample of the detail, and where totals do not agree, all the detail relevant to that section is checked in order to find the reason for the discrepancy. Care must be taken to ensure that not only the printed output is correct but also carried-forward file data remaining on magnetic tape or disks.

Parallel running is usually operated for a few processing cycles of an application, the actual number being dependent upon its complexity and the data volumes involved. After the first cycle, only the results from the old system are distributed to the users, the new system's results being employed purely for checking purposes. If these prove to be satisfactory, the computer's output is distributed after subsequent processing cycles while the old system's results are held in reserve in case of dispute. In situations where the computer's output has different contents or layout from the old results, both sets of documents are distributed to internal users together with an accompanying explanatory note.

The major problem with parallel running is, of course, its inherent duplication of work, most of which falls upon the user department staff in that they are not only doing their normal work but are also concerned with preparing the source data documentation for the d.p. system and then checking its output.

Phased changeover—This is similar to parallel running except that initially only a portion of the data is run in parallel on the d.p. system, customers' accounts in one area for instance. During the processing cycles that follow, more sections of the data are added to the new system, and in each case the old system runs in parallel for one processing cycle only. Thus the old system is phased out gradually and at each stage it is quite practical to check and compare the corresponding outputs before distribution, the over-all extra work involved is generally less than with parallel running.

Stage-by-stage changeover—In this context a stage can be regarded as a routine or a complete application, and this method is not so much an alternative as complementary to the methods described above. It is, in actuality, the arrangement adopted by nearly all companies in relation to their major applications, usually starting with the payroll, then stock recording, and so on. Stage-by-stage changeover can also be applied to the routines within an application. The most important feature of this method is the need to dovetail later stages without disruption of those already functioning. A typical stage-by-stage changeover of a basic accounting system would be:

Stage 1 Preparation of invoices from despatch notes.
Stage 2 Preparation of sales analyses from invoiced items.
Stage 3 Updating of sales ledger accountants from invoice totals.
Stage 4 Preparation of statements from the ledger accounts.
Stage 5 Automatic preparation of overdue account reminders, and so on.

Chapter 7   Basic Accounting Functions by Computer

7.1   A typical data processing system

The previous chapters in this book have described in some detail how d.p. systems are investigated and designed, what machinery is used, and the procedures and problems associated with the implementation of such systems.

The present chapter shows an outline of a typical d.p. system—what inputs are handled—what processing is done—what reports are produced. It is not the intention to describe technically advanced applications but to demonstrate the basic or foundation activities of the organisation. Because of the probable background of the majority of readers, the accounting applications are described in the most detail but it should be emphasised that the principles of data processing discussed in this book apply to all types of applications and not just accounting ones.

The pattern of this chapter is intended to show how the usual accounting functions, e.g. ledger keeping, credit control, budgetary control, expenditure analysis, final account preparation and so on, might be dealt with by a d.p. system. The description is not of one particular firm but would be appropriate to a moderate sized manufacturing concern of 500–1,000 employees. Particular facets, such as batch control, file contents or the contents of a particular report, are dealt with in greater detail when they illustrate a particularly interesting point but the general aim is to put the detailed systems material of the earlier chapters into perspective.

The d.p. system to be described is an integrated one encompassing; Payroll, Sales Accounting, Stock Control, Plant Register, Nominal Ledger and Budgetary Control with the associated Cash, Reserves, and Journal adjustments. Before considering the system flowcharts covering each facet of the system, some factors which affect all or most sub-systems are discussed.

7.2 Accounts and cost centre codes

Some handwritten and semi-mechanised accounting systems manage without defined accounts codes. Such informality is not possible with d.p. systems and well publicised, comprehensive codes are essential.

The nominal ledger account codes which are necessary for the system described in this chapter are three digit codes, grouped into three broad categories viz.

000–229   BALANCE SHEET ITEMS including all forms of assets, inventories, investments, reserves and provisions.

300–599   EXPENSE ITEMS including wages, salaries, office expenses, selling and distribution expenses, direct and indirect materials.

600–999   REVENUE ITEMS including product sales, rebates, containers, commissions.

The various cash and bank accounts are included in the nominal ledger which thus becomes self balancing.

Financial schedule codes

One of the main products of the accounting applications to be described are the Financial Schedules, which are produced monthly. These schedules include; the monthly balance sheet, profit and loss account, and supporting schedules which give greater detail of various assets, expenditures, and revenues. To facilitate the automatic collation, summation, and production of these schedules, each nominal account has associated with it a schedule and line number which is a cross referencing code to the point of original entry in the monthly schedules.

As examples of this, consider the following nominal ledger accounts:

NOMINAL LEDGER ACCOUNTS CODE	NOMINAL LEDGER ACCOUNT DESCRIPTION	SCHEDULE/LINE REFERENCE
005	Machinery	5/10
006	Lorries	5/12
007	Equipment	5/13
351	Fuel oil	12/7
352	Coke	12/7
353	Electricity	12/7
660	Sales-Retail products-Home-Third parties	4/10
661	Sales-Retail products-Home-Group Cos.	3/10

In the examples shown above the original points of entry into the monthly schedules would be:

Schedule 5, which shows details of tangible assets giving last year's position, current year additions and disposals, and the current situations as at the month end.

Schedule 12, which shows details of expenditure for the current period under analysed headings. The three examples above are in the nominal account range 350–359—Power and Water.

Schedule 4, which shows details of sales to third parties and, together with many other account codes, shows Domestic and Export Sales.

Schedule 3, which shows details of total sales both within the Group and to third parties.

In most cases many other nominal account codes will be combined with the few examples shown to make up the appropriate line of the particular schedule. In each of the above cases only the point of original entry into the financial schedules is shown. The print program producing the schedules contains the codes showing the hierarchical relationships between the various schedules.

As an example, the fixed asset accounts shown (005, 006 and 007) together with the other twenty or so categories of fixed assets appear, suitably analysed, on Schedule 5—Tangible Assets. The totals of Schedule 5 appear as three summary figures on Schedule 1—monthly balance sheet as shown in Fig. 7.1.

Cost centre codes

In addition to the nature of the expense or the type of asset or revenue, the location of the expenditure or asset is of importance for operating statements, costing and budgetary control. Therefore a cost centre coding system must exist. For reporting and summarising purposes a four-digit code is used which serves three levels, i.e. location information at factory, department, and individual cost centre level.

Thus, code 2109 could represent Department 2, cost centre 109, and as cost centre codes 100–300 are reserved for 'A' factory, the full meaning of the code is department 2, cost centre 109, 'A' factory. This coding structure, by appropriate programming, will permit analysis to cost centres, the grouping of cost centres into departments, and of departments into factories.

7.3 Batching and batch control

All data capable of being totalled is batched and totalled prior to entry to the d.p. system. A rigorous batch control system is applied throughout the whole movement and processing of the batch, i.e. from the originating department, through the control section (Section 9.2) and data preparation to the computer itself.

Each user department is issued with a master list of batch numbers which must be used sequentially. If a batch number is missed the computer is programmed to report the fact. The user department batches the data, calculates one or more batch totals as appropriate for the data, and attaches a batch slip to each batch. The batch slip shows batch number, batch total(s), data type, date and department code.

After logging the batch into the control section, the batch is passed for punching and verification. If an error is found, or a document is indecipherable, the batch is returned to the originating department and the return noted in the control section log.

On entry of the batch into the computer the batch number is checked for sequence and the control total(s) are calculated and compared with the batch control card. The control account entry in the computer maintained accounts is generated automatically from the batch control card, provided that the batch is correct. If there is a disagreement over the batch totals (or any type of error is found) the details of the whole batch are printed out to assist clerical scrutiny. Some batches are self-balancing, e.g. those containing journal vouchers where the debit and credit entries must be equal and both must equal the batch total.

For standard financial transactions, i.e. non-journal items, the double entry for each transaction or group of transactions is automatically generated by the program on entry of the source transaction. This reduces input volumes and ensures accuracy. In the case of accrued items the program generates an appropriate entry of opposite sign for the next period's accounts.

7.4 Audit trail

The system must be acceptable to the organisation's auditors so, as one of the audit and control considerations (Chapter 9), a good audit trail is provided. The full audit trail is not printed automatically but can be printed in part or completely, on demand. Each user department has a code, and each source document has a type code and serial number. These details are stored on the

Line No.	Assets	Current year	As at	Detail on schedule
	Tangible assets			
1	— at accumulated cost	x x x x x	x x x x x	5
2	— less accumulated depreciation	x x x x x	x x x x x	5
3	— book value	x x x x x	x x x x x	5

Balance sheet as at .... SCHEDULE I

FIG. 7.1 Example of relationship of schedules

audit file so that the original document has a unique cross-reference. This part of the system provides the historical audit trail which is retained until after the annual audit. By keeping the detailed audit information in this way computer printout is reduced. Indeed, particular care should be taken in the design of d.p. systems not to produce voluminous printouts purely for auditing purposes.

However, some information which is used internally and which can be used for audit purposes is printed out after each computer run. This includes; number of correct batches processed, control totals of correct batches, details of batches rejected, and after the processing is complete, an over-all ledger reconciliation of the form:

> Opening balance at beginning of year
> + Movements to end of previous month
> + This month's movements to date
> = New balance

7.5 Open item ledgers

Using handwritten and accounting machine systems a feature of personal ledger accounts is the account balance. The production of this balance is an integral part of the processing in such systems but the net balance of the account is only meaningful in relation to the current up-to-date position. Other information is of importance in the accounting system. Examples of other required data are; sales/purchases by period and cumulatively, cash paid and received, returns inward and outward, and the ageing of account balances.

Much of this information when using clerical and mechanised systems has to be gained from other records, or by subsequent analysis. Using a d.p. system there are considerable advantages in integrating as many records as possible. A way of doing this is to maintain personal accounts, as far as is possible, in open item fashion rather than merely bringing forward net balances.

A simple comparison of the two systems in double entry form, is as follows:

NET BALANCE SYSTEM A/C No. 905621 @ 31.5.72				OPEN ITEM SYSTEM A/C No. 905621 @ 31.5.72			
		Debits	*Credits*			*Debits*	*Credits*
01 May	Bal. B/F	100.20		At 01 May			
11 May	Inv. 8527	68.59		30 Jan.	Inv. 6306	20.60	
05 May	Chq.		32.80	16 Feb.	Inv. 6521	67.40	
23 May	Inv. 9851	73.00		20 Mar.	Inv. 7957	12.20	
		────	────	11 May	Inv. 8527	68.59	
		241.79	32.80	05 May	Chq. 1062		32.80
		────	────	23 May	Inv. 9851	73.00	
						────	────
						241.79	32.80
						────	────

	Debits	Credits			Debits	Credits
At 01 Jun.						
16 Feb.	Inv. 6521				67.40	
11 May	Inv. 8527				68.59	
23 May	Inv. 9851				73.00	

The above example clearly represents only the simplest situation and problems arise where payments do not match individual invoices. This problem also exists under the net balance system. The net balance system 'overcomes' this problem at the expense of other necessary information, e.g. the ageing of balances for credit control. One solution to the problem is to use the calculating power of the computer and its vast filing capacity to maintain the data-base. That is to say, maintain the usual ledger information plus any other required control and statistical information, on an open item basis yet produce most documentation on a net balance brought forward basis.

Periodically, full file printouts can be produced, automatically or on request, to facilitate clearing of unmatched cash or small balances.

If the data-base is maintained at the item level and the ageing of balances on statements involves only the totalling of detailed movements, then the totals themselves are not held directly on file but are generated according to parameter requests. This arrangement gives flexibility in that statements can be prepared showing aged movements for 1, 2, 3, 4 ... previous periods as required, and a net balance brought forward for all earlier periods.

7.6 Month end closing

Using earlier processing methods a particular problem is that of striking balances at month ends. Because of the time overlaps, some movements for subsequent accounting periods are available before all the movements for the current accounting period are cleared and posted. In view of this, it is quite normal procedure to refrain from posting new entries until all the old entries have been cleared. Apart from the control and clerical filing problems that this practice encourages, it causes the work flow to be uneven and is a contributory factor to month end peaks.

With a properly designed d.p. system this problem can be largely overcome. If the date is incorporated into each transaction entry and the computer is correctly programmed to keep the accounting periods separate, transactions can be entered into the system as they become available. The computer will ensure that only entries relating to past periods are taken into account for nominal ledger summaries, budgetary control, final account schedules, statements and remittance advices, yet will retain complete records of the entries relating to future periods. The above method is an example of a basic data processing principle which should be incorporated wherever possible, i.e. let the computer do the basic filing, re-arrangement and calculation. It does this

sort of work far better than people provided, of course, it is correctly programmed to start with.

7.7 A typical computer-based accounting system

Figures 7.2 to 7.10 show the system flowcharts for an integrated accounting
system. Each flowchart is largely self-explanatory and uses the symbols shown
in Fig. 5.4.

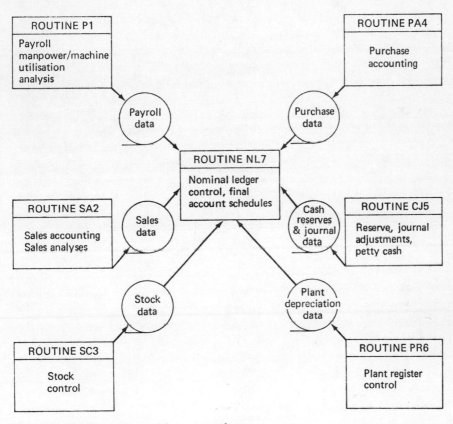

FIG. 7.2 Main routines and interconnections

Main routines and interconnections (Fig. 7.2)

Each of the functional routines, sales accounting, payroll and so on, produces
posting data to update the nominal ledger. This data is written by the functional routines on to magnetic tape during the individual processing runs.
The tapes produced can be used to update the nominal ledger progressively
throughout the month or, where the volume of transactions is small, at the
month end.

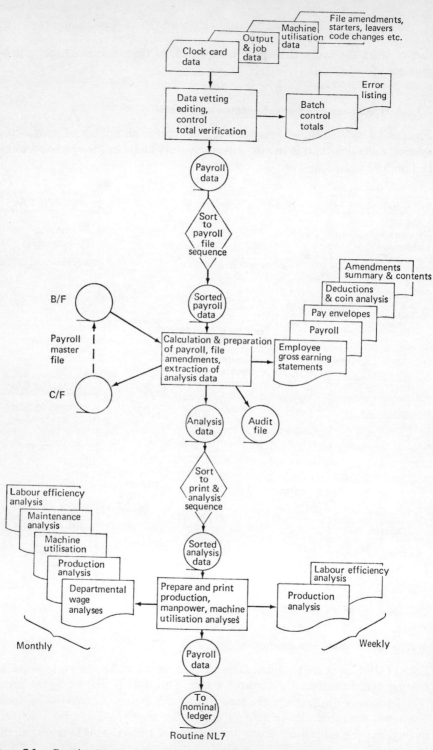

Fɪɢ. 7.3 Routine P1—payroll analysis—simplified systems flowchart

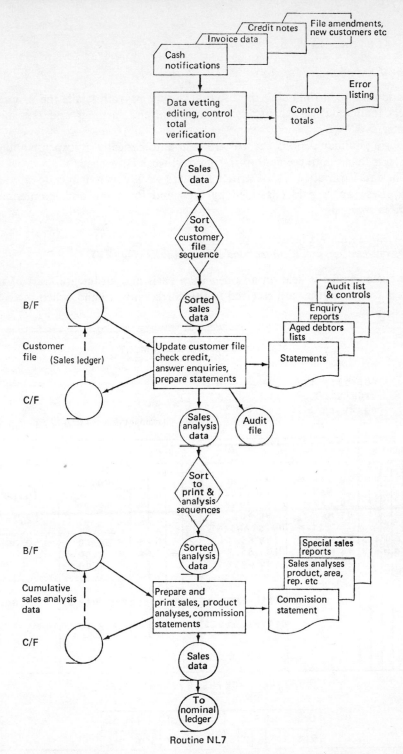

Fig. 7.4   Routine SA2—sales accounting, credit control, sales analysis—simplified systems flowchart

Payroll and analysis (Fig. 7.3)

In addition to maintaining the usual statutory payroll details the program caters for holiday pay, coin analysis and year-end earnings and tax statements.

During holiday periods, records are held automatically in suspense and no action is taken until the appropriate payroll week is reached.

The data for routine NL7 is written forward weekly on to magnetic tape and comprises; wages paid (classified by type and location), and maintenance services charged.

Sales accounting, credit control and sales analysis (Fig. 7.4)

The customer file is held on an open item basis and an integral part of the system is relating the cash received to the correct invoice and, when the cash

```
                ACCOUNTS COPY — STATEMENT

        POLYDATA LTD
        HIGH ST.
        BRAMWICH
                                    Statement date:  31/05/72

  Trans. Ref                        Cash Ref.

             30 JAN 72   INV 6306              20.60
             05 MAY 72   CHQ 1062                            20.60
             20 MAR 72   INV 7957              12.20
             05 MAY 72   CHQ 1062                            12.20
                ITEMS   OUTSTANDING
 1 5 0 6 c s 16 FEB 72   INV 6521     2 9 5 4  67.40        60.00
 1 5 0 6 c 3 11 MAY 72   INV 8527     2 9 5 4  68.59✓
             23 MAY 72   INV 9851              73.00

             TOTAL CASH RECEIVED DURING MAY              32.80

             NET BALANCE                       208.99


                THREE MONTHS OVERDUE 67.40

        Dept/Batch Ref    Cash Total    Lines
        9 3 1 5 6 2 8  £    128.59p    0 2
```

FIG. 7.5   Accounts copy of customer's statement

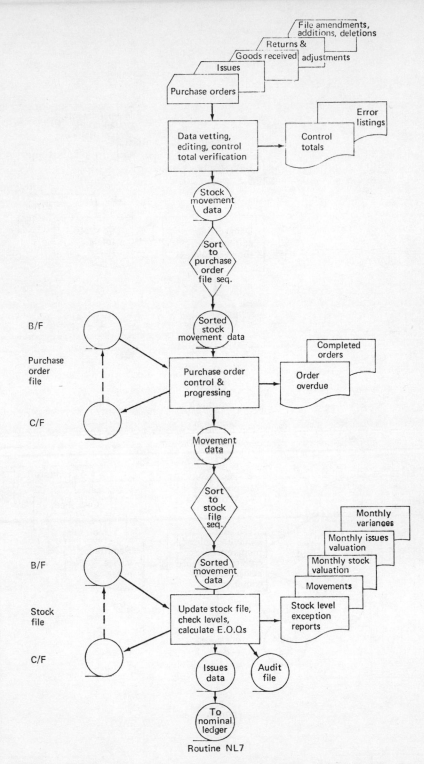

Fig. 7.6   Routine SC3—stock control, purchase order control—simplified systems flow-chart

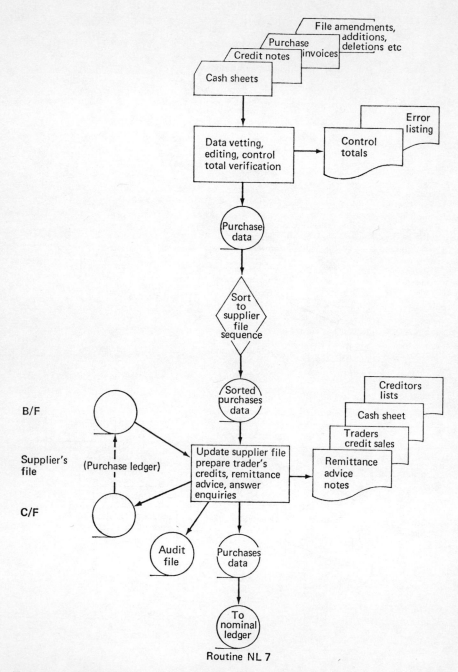

FIG. 7.7   Routine PA4—purchase ledger and purchase accounting—simplified systems flowchart

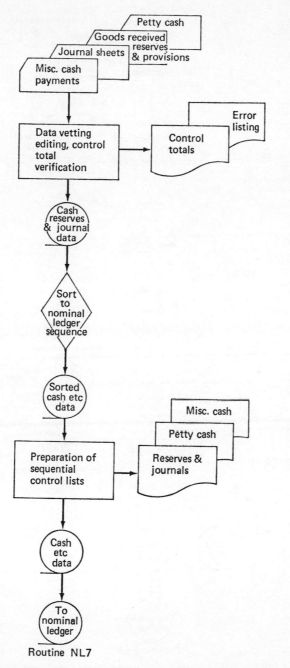

FIG. 7.8 Routine CJ5—cash reserves and journal adjustments—simplified systems flow-chart

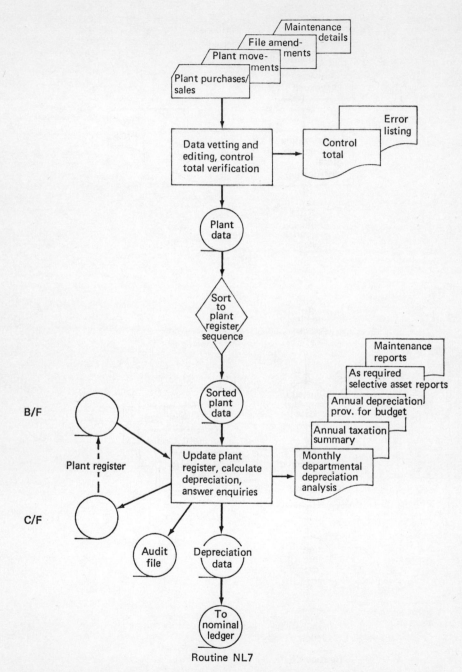

FIG. 7.9 Routine PR6—maintenance of plant register and depreciation records—simplified systems flowchart

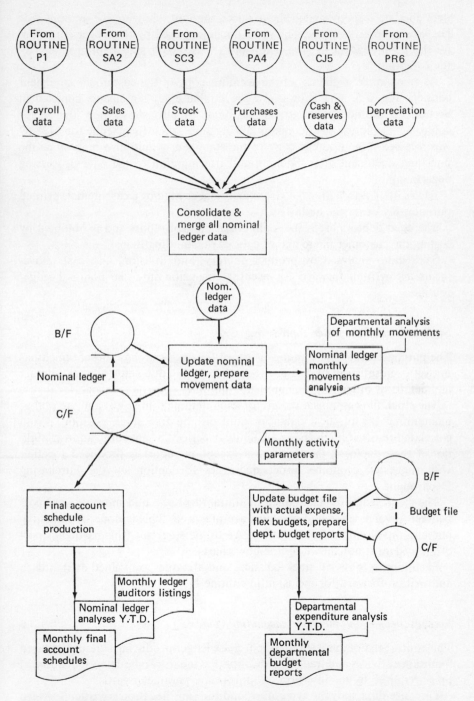

FIG. 7.10 Routine NL7—nominal ledger, budgetary control, monthly and annual accounts—simplified systems flowchart

item does not exactly match the invoiced amount, showing the amount that has been paid on account. The main document used by the ledger controller for this purpose is the accounts copy of the customer's statement produced by the computer.

As an example of the use of the accounts copy of the customer's statement consider Fig. 7.5. This shows how the double entry statements depicted in Section 7.5 would appear to the customer. It also shows how the ledger controller would use the document during June when the cheque for £128.59 was received. The accounts copy of the statement would also be used as the punching document after batching and transmission to the data processing department.

Each settled transaction, i.e. an invoice item cleared by a cash item, is printed out monthly on to the audit list.

The aged debtors list is the main credit control report and is obtained by sorting the customer file to age of debt of outstanding items.

Sales data, analysed by product, factory, and division, and cash movements are written forward for eventual inclusion into the nominal ledger routines.

Stock and purchase order control (Fig. 7.6)

The purchase order file contains a record for each purchase order which has not yet been satisfied. Orders are controlled by the due delivery week number and details of orders overdue are listed until the order is satisfied.

The stock file contains a record for each item held in stores and, as well as maintaining the physical balances, controls the free stock position. From calculated re-order levels (based on delivery periods, usage rates, and variabilities of these factors), the stock level exception report is produced together with suggested economic order quantities for action by the Purchasing Department.

The stock ledger is maintained at standard prices, and monthly variances between invoice value and standard are prepared. This is done by matching purchase invoice data from routine PA4 to the stock file (this particular part of the system is not shown on the flow charts).

Each month, physical stock balances and all issues are valued at standard, and written forward for inclusion in routine NL7.

Purchase ledger and purchase accounting (Fig. 7.7)

This routine maintains a standard purchase ledger producing suitably itemised remittance advices and traders credit slips. Payments can be delayed or speeded up as required by the insertion of appropriate parameter cards.

Purchase data showing type of expenditure and location is written forward for use in routine NL7.

Cash, reserves, and journal adjustments (Fig. 7.8)

This routine deals with the consolidation of the many incidental reserves and adjustments prior to their entry into the main nominal ledger routine.

Plant register and depreciation records (Fig. 7.9)

The plant register can be controlled by asset number, nominal account code and cost centre code, and reports can be produced at any of these levels. Depreciation is calculated monthly, depending on the number of working days, and written forward for inclusion in the nominal ledger routines.

Control data on planned maintenance schedules is prepared and comparisons made between planned maintenance and actual maintenance carried out.

Nominal ledger and budgetary control (Fig. 7.10)

As described in Section 7.2, the nominal ledger is arranged in three main sections—balance sheet, expenditure and revenue items. Upon consolidation of the data from the six supporting routines, the nominal ledger becomes self balancing. After the updating of the nominal ledger the account balances are grouped according to their schedule/line numbers, for inclusion in the monthly accounts.

The budget file contains the budgeted expenses for each expenditure type for each cost centre. The expenditure budget is stored in the form of a fixed portion and a variable element. According to the monthly activity parameters, the budget is flexed and compared with the actual expenditures derived from the nominal ledger which retains the account history by month and by cost centre.

Chapter 8 Financial Aspects of Data Processing Systems

The financial aspects of d.p. systems have, on occasions, been neglected in the pursuit of technical excellence for its own sake. This is undoubtedly an aspect of computer operations which could benefit from the accountant's scrutiny.

There is a definite need to subject d.p. systems to the same scrutiny of costs in relation to benefits as any other sphere of commercial activity. Indeed, it could be argued that a closer scrutiny is necessary because of the very substantial sums involved, both for equipment and personnel.

Because of the esoteric nature of some d.p. systems, the aura of sophistication and the all pervasive jargon, there has been on occasions, a reluctance to ask basic questions such as, 'Will it be a worthwhile financial proposition to install a computer?' or, 'Is our d.p. system producing the benefits which we intended?'

These two questions indicate the two broad areas where financial appraisals occur. Firstly, before the decision is taken to install a d.p. system, and subsequently, after installation, the monitoring of costs and benefits so as to ensure that planned benefits are not frittered away by unplanned cost increases.

An objective, and indeed, hard-headed approach is necessary but the approach should not be a reactionary one. Care should be taken to cultivate a profit-conscious attitude rather than a purely cost-conscious one. It is the margin between benefits and costs which is significant not the absolute amount of either factor.

There should be early recognition that there are many subjective elements present in these appraisals, particularly with regard to the appraisal prior to installation. This is, of course, nothing new as all decision-making relates to the future, therefore forecasts and estimates are always necessary.

8.1 Appraisal prior to installation

The financial appraisal at this stage is variously termed an investment appraisal, a project appraisal or a capital expenditure appraisal. This is undoubtedly the most significant stage and capital expenditure decisions are probably the most important that management has to take. Usually such decisions are taken at board level and it is the accountant's task to present the salient factors clearly and concisely so that a rational decision, in the light of the information available, may be made. Of course, boards of directors do sometimes make irrational decisions in spite of adequate information, but that is another story!

This section is not concerned with *which* computer should be chosen, that is, the technical process of selection based on speeds, capacities, software support etc., but covers the appraisal prior to the technical selection, i.e. should *any* computer be chosen?

It is important for the accountant to be involved in this appraisal in order to ensure that the matter is treated as a commercial decision, which it undoubtedly is, and not a technical decision. Although the accountant will be intimately involved in the appraisal and will probably collate and present the information, it should be recognised that many other people in the organisation will also participate. Close liaison between the members of the team undertaking the investigation, functional and line management who will be affected by the proposed d.p. system, and the accountant, is absolutely vital if a comprehensive analysis is to be undertaken.

Discounted cash flow

The method of treatment of a proposed computer installation as a commercial investment appraisal is given in some detail later in this chapter and the appraisal method employed is based on the use of discounted cash flow (DCF) techniques.

DCF techniques are now generally recognised as providing a rational means of appraising potential investment projects, but no claim is made for infallibility. No method of appraisal can reduce decision-making to a mechanical process, and the uncertainties inherent in the majority of investment appraisals make the exercise of judgement and specific experience an essential part of the appraisal process.

DCF methods are based on a consideration of the cash flows, not book 'profits', of an investment and of the timings of these cash flows. There are two basic DCF methods, the DCF return and Net Present Value (NPV). The latter method is used in the case study in Section 8.6 so only NPV will be described.

Because of the usage factor of money (for individuals, this is called interest), the uncertainties of the future and the affects of inflation, it is generally accepted that money has a value which varies according to the time when it is received. That is, money received now is worth more than money received in the future. In an investment project money will be spent and received at various times in the future and the purpose of the NPV method of investment appraisal is to reduce to a common basis, i.e. its value at the present time, these various cash receipts and expenditures. To do this it is necessary to calculate some rate of discount which will be used to reduce (discount) the future sums to their present day value. This rate of discount is generally termed the 'cost of capital' of the organisation. The calculation of cost of capital is a complex subject outside the scope of this book but interested readers are advised to consult one of the many texts specifically concerned with investment appraisal [13].

Tables are available in such textbooks which give the factors for various discounting rates over numerous time periods, and all that is necessary to convert future cash flows into present values is to multiply the cash flow of the appropriate period by the factor for that period.

As an example, consider the following simple project being considered in a company with a cost of capital of 10 per cent.

PROJECT Z involves a cash outlay now of £9,000 and is expected to earn net cash inflows of £1,500, £3,000, £3,000, £2,500 and £2,500 in years 1 to 5, respectively. (Note: it is conventional to assume that cash flows are received at the end of each year in one amount and most discount tables are calculated accordingly.)

NPV CALCULATION—PROJECT Z

Period	Cash flow, £	Discount factor @ 10%	Present value, £
0	− 9,000	1·0	− 9,000
1	+ 1,500	0·909	+ 1,363
2	+ 3,000	0·826	+ 2,478
3	+ 3,000	0·751	+ 2,253
4	+ 2,500	0·683	+ 1,707
5	+ 2,500	0·621	+ 1,552

NPV of project £ + 353

The interpretation of this positive value of NPV is that Project Z represents a capital gain as yet unrealised and that, ignoring risk and uncertainty, the project should be accepted assuming that the capital is available at a cost of 10 per cent.

The above brief example shows the basic principle of DCF and of the NPV method in particular but is clearly unrealistically simple. A proper investment appraisal will involve a detailed consideration of the amounts and timings of cash outflows, the amounts and timings of the cash inflows derived from the benefits of the proposed investment, the taxation consequences of expenditures and operating surpluses and indeed, a consideration of every consequence of the investment which effects the cash flow of the organisation.

It will be apparent that evaluating any investment proposal involves fore-casts, estimates and the exercise of judgement. This is inevitable because all decision-making relates to future periods which obviously contain a larger or smaller element of uncertainty. The uncertainty inherent in the data is no excuse for failure to make anything other than a comprehensive and detailed appraisal using all the information available, and to use the most rational investment appraisal techniques for the analysis of the data gathered.

8.2 Data processing system investment appraisal

The following sections describe the factors which should be considered in the appraisal of a proposed d.p. system.

The report of the team undertaking the systems investigation and system design will provide a considerable amount of information on the applications to be covered, the equipment required initially and in the future, the staff involved, and the benefits expected.

All incremental effects of the d.p. system need consideration. That is, whatever changes in cash outflows or inflows take place on the introduction of the d.p. system must be brought into the appraisal. For example, if the installation of the computer necessitated moving an existing department, not only the obvious installation costs of the computer must be considered but also the removal and resiting costs associated with the transfer.

Care should be taken to consider items in detail and over-all approximations such as, 'installation costs are about 8 per cent of the purchase price of the computer', should be avoided. There are two reasons for this. Over-all percentages and approximations are not necessarily very accurate and make the estimation of the timing of cash flows more difficult. Secondly, if a detailed analysis is carried out and documented, the resulting information provides a first class basis for the budgetary control of costs after installation.

The costs of d.p. systems, i.e. the cash outflows which will be used in the investment appraisal, will be considered first. It cannot be emphasised too strongly that the timings as well as the cash amounts must be carefully gauged.

The majority of the items below are capable of verification but many estimates are still involved.

8.3 Costs—cash flows and timings

The main items of cost involved in the installation of d.p. systems are set out below. For convenience they have been grouped into broad categories but the items are not necessarily mutually exclusive.

Equipment and installation—cash flows and timings

Computer main frame.
Computer main frame additions.

Peripherals.
Additions to peripherals.
Data preparation and conversion equipment.
Data links.
Terminals and visual displays.
Initial stocks of magnetic tapes/disks.
Delivery charges.
Installation including:
  Removal and resiting of existing departments.
  Demolition costs and structural alterations.
  Floors, partitions, ceilings.
  Lighting.
  Sound proofing and double glazing.
  Air conditioning and ducting.
  Stabilised electrical supplies.
  Standby power equipment.
Magnetic recording media storage.
Data processing staff accommodation and furniture.
Ancillary equipment, racks, trolleys, trays, etc.
Output handling equipment, bursters, guillotines, etc.
Intercom and telephone systems.
Architect/design/engineering fees.
Penalty/proceeds from disposal/realisation of existing equipment, when
  redundant.
Exchange losses, if currency conversion is involved.

Personnel, recruitment, training—cash flows and timings

Consultant's fees.
Salaries of:
  Data processing manager(s).
  Systems analysts and programmers.
  Operators and librarians.
  Control section staff.
  Data preparation staff.
  Messengers and clerical assistants.
Staff advertising, recruitment and selection costs.
Relocation expenses.
Travelling and out of pocket expenses.
Overtime and shift working allowances.
Pension fund and other additional payments.
Training costs, course fees, materials, travelling, etc.

Note: This area of cost is particularly volatile and due allowance must be made for staff turnover, the continual re-training of new and existing staff and realistic salary progressions.

Development costs—cash flows and timings

Consultant's fees.

Program testing charges prior to installation of own computer, i.e. over and above the computer supplier's free allowance.

Contract programming fees.

Payments for software and/or packages (not from manufacturer).

File conversion costs.

General staff, i.e. non data processing, training and data processing appreciation courses.

Customer/supplier/d.p. system user-training and informative literature.

Parallel running costs, if any.

Any data preparation costs not included in staff salaries or operating costs.

Note: In addition to the usual difficulties of estimating the *amount* of the cash flows involved, the *timings* of the development costs raise particular problems. In general, it would be fair to say that development costs and particularly the time for development are usually sadly underestimated. Quite apart from the additional costs involved, this has the effect of delaying planned benefits.

Operating costs—cash flows and timings

Salaries, already detailed, are excluded.

Consumable materials, stationery, ribbons, cards, paper tape.

Replacement and addition of magnetic tape and disks.

Reconditioning of magnetic tapes and disks.

Engineering maintenance (labour and spares) on computer main frame, peripherals, ancillary equipment, and air conditioning.

Building maintenance.

Rent, heating and cleaning costs.

Electricity costs.

Cost of standby arrangements on bureau and/or other user's installation.

Any rental costs of small items such as data preparation equipment.

Rentals of modems and communication systems.

Telephone and line charges.

Insurance premiums of which there are four categories:

Replacement costs of computer, buildings and general equipment.

Replacement costs of specially written programs.

Costs involved in production of work at alternative installations if computer is destroyed or damaged.

Normal loss of profits.

It is not claimed that the above lists are exhaustive and it is obvious that not all the items apply to every d.p. system. However, the lists do indicate the depth of detail that must be considered not only for the purpose of the investment appraisal but to enable detailed management plans to be evolved for the implementation of the d.p. system.

Although some estimation is involved in the items in the foregoing lists, little real difficulty will be experienced compared with the problems involved in arriving at the benefits of the system, which are discussed in the next section.

8.4   Benefits—cash flows and timings

Unfortunately, some people seem to imply that having a d.p. system is so obvious a benefit, *per se*, that detailed consideration of the benefits arising from the system is not necessary. An alternative strategy, which must also be vigorously rebuffed, is that a d.p. system is such a special beast that no form of appraisal is possible.

Detailed appraisals are considered necessary and are carried out for all other types of investment projects, e.g. new products, new factories, acquisitions of companies, etc. etc. Why not for d.p. systems?

A common argument is that many of the benefits are 'intangibles', i.e. such things as better management information, closer control and faster production of reports. There is no doubt that benefits from these results of a d.p. system do arise but it is the authors' contention that if a benefit is so intangible that its long and/or short term relationship to profit cannot be estimated even in very broad terms, then it is not a benefit at all and should be totally disregarded. It appears to be common practice, at least amongst those who have a vested interest in the installation of d.p. systems, to shy away from any attempts to quantify intangible benefits yet to attach inordinate weight to these in assessing whether or not to install a d.p. system.

It is a salutary exercise for all concerned to attempt to quantify the intangibles. This forces everyone involved to give detailed consideration to the benefits of the system, thus bringing home to top management who are, after all, the ultimate decision takers, the values which are being ascribed to such matters as, for instance, the advantage of receiving an operating statement three days earlier.

Because of the far-reaching nature of a d.p. systems investigation, it is considered a good time to question the necessity of any work being done before attention is paid to how such work will be carried out by the system. The objective of each area of the company's work must be considered afresh and the likely benefits reappraised.

The ultimate test of a d.p. system is the comparison of the costs of the system with the benefits resulting from the work produced by the system. It is not merely a comparison of the costs of carrying out work by existing methods and the costs of carrying out the same work by the proposed d.p. system.

Using this approach it will be clear that statements such as 'A computer working a single shift cannot be profitable' or, 'The breakeven point of computer usage is 1½ shift working, therefore as our computer is on 2 shifts we must be profitable', are at the best, only half-truths and at the worst, positively misleading. Although it is self-evident that the cost per line of output or per job will fall as the utilisation of the computer increases, this does not automatically mean that the installation is or will be profitable.

It is worth repeating the fundamental point made in the first chapter. Does the d.p. system merely produce the record of results quicker, or more comprehensively, or does it affect the results?

Some of the benefits of d.p. systems are more readily ascertained than others, e.g. clerical cost savings brought about by the replacement of a section of keyboard accounting macl.ine operators by a d.p. system. Even in such cases care should still be taken to consider the true incremental effects of the new situation.

The calculation of the values of benefits that are expected is not primarily the task of the accountant, although his advice may be sought. These values should be derived by the team carrying out the Systems Investigation and Design in association with line and functional management. The estimation of values is individual to each organisation and each application and is, of necessity, a mainly subjective process. The best general advice that can be given is to express the benefits expected, stage by stage, in the units appropriate to the application. This should be done in as detailed a manner as possible and only at the end are the units to be converted into financial terms.

For example, assume that part of a production control system is to be handled by the d.p. system. Certain benefits are expected and after detailed consideration the Production Controller, the Works Manager, and the Systems Analyst agreed the following as being the most likely results of the d.p. system.

1 By faster processing, and a more comprehensive and up-to-date database, the average time for the production of works documentation, routing instructions, schedules etc. would reduce from 10 working days to 8 working days.
2 Better routing through the factory would reduce work in progress from an average of 25 days equivalent production to 20 days equivalent production.
3 The ability to reflect specification changes more quickly and comprehensively would result in a reduction in reworks from the present 4 per cent of production to 3 per cent of production.
4 More rational routing would make internal transport 15 per cent more effective and would thus result in a reduction of 5 personnel and associated truck hire charges.

When these and similar such estimates have been made, they require to be valued to bring to a common financial basis. It is at this stage that the assistance of the accounting department is required in order to provide previous costs, rates, and revenues so that the best possible estimate can be made of the values of the benefits expected.

Typical of the general area in which benefits might occur are the following.

Personnel savings

On occasions, particularly when a high volume repetitive clerical application is involved, some savings are expected due to clerical staff, machine operators and record keepers being replaced by the d.p. system. In general, these types of savings do not appear to be made quite as readily as was anticipated in the early days of computers. The cost savings that may be involved relate to salary and general support expenditure and care should be taken over the timings of any anticipated savings, redundancy payments and the tendency for staff to be absorbed with other departments.

Accommodation/equipment savings

If the introduction of the d.p. system releases accommodation and/or equipment and the facilities thus released can be utilised effectively, there are likely to be some benefits from reductions (or reduced increases) in rent or hire charges.

Speedier report production

It is likely that one of the advantages claimed from the proposed d.p. system will be the earlier production of invoices, statements, schedules, analyses of all types, works documentation, control and operating statements, etc., and it is true that this is an undoubted benefit. Unfortunately, the benefits are not always easy to quantify in financial terms although some effects are fairly obvious. For example, assume that the earlier production of invoices and statements results in an estimated reduction of 5 days in the collection of debts. If debtors previously averaged 60 days to settle, the estimated time saved represents an $8\frac{1}{2}$ per cent reduction in debtors who, it will be assumed, average £500,000. For a company operating on an overdraft of 8 per cent per annum the annual cash flow benefit, before tax considerations, is £3,400.

Greater accuracy

Because of the precision with which a computer obeys a program, greater accuracy of all output is likely, provided that the accuracy of source data can be maintained.

The benefits to be estimated here are the reduction or elimination of the losses previously incurred through inaccuracies. Some data on previous inaccuracies may be gained by carrying out in depth sample checks on invoice extensions, item pricings, costing calculations, estimates for new jobs, or in whatever area is to be implemented. Information may already be available from analyses by cause, of goods returned, items rejected by inspection or reworks in the factory.

More detailed statistics

With the more comprehensive data-base and the fast processing speeds that are possible with a d.p. system, the production of more detailed analyses and statistics becomes feasible, and this is a common feature of d.p. systems. The benefits that are derived relate to the uses which are made of the reports and analyses by their recipients. Typical of the analyses and statistics prepared, are; sales analyses by area, product, discount group, outlet, representative, etc.; stock analyses by material classification, age, rate of turnover, value, usage patterns, etc.; debtor analyses by type of customer, age, credit limit, value of sales and method of payment.

Quantification of benefits in many such cases is extremely difficult but presumably some advantage is expected from the statistics, so it is not unreasonable to question the managers about their expectations.

Operational control

A major advantage associated with a well designed d.p. system is the greater operational control that is possible over such matters as stocks, stock turnover, reordering, debtors and credit control, production control and scheduling. The advantage that the d.p. system has in these areas is that a more comprehensive and consistent view can be taken of the situation than would be possible with a clerical system.

Because of the high calculating speeds and rapid access to past records, the scope for Operational Research (OR) techniques is greater and invariably some OR techniques are included in most large scale d.p. systems. Quite apart from the advantages associated with the treatment of operations, there is the additional benefit that management's time is saved by not having to deal personally with standard situations. Through a properly designed exception-reporting system management can be notified of conditions that need individual attention.

Probably most of the measurable benefits from d.p. systems stem from closer control over operations, and here quantification is relatively easy. For example, the table in Fig. 8.1 [slightly adapted from Table 2 of 'Business information systems', *Data Processing* (May–June, 1969)] gives some of the benefits gained by the Honeywell Micro Switch Division from the progressive implementation of a d.p. system.

	Honeywell Micro Switch Division Operational Benefits			
Year	On time deliveries %	Sales/stock ratio	Adverse production cost variances %	Clerical and DP costs % of sales
1952	58	4.3	24	3.7
1956	80	4.2	16	3.6
1961	93	4.4	6	3.7
1963	96	5.2	1	3.3
1966	97	6.2	1	2.8

Fig. 8.1

Scientific methods

In most clerical systems there is not the calculating power or time available to carry out extensive analyses of data or to optimise complex situations. A d.p. system enables more scientific methods to be used usually through well established statistical and/or OR techniques. Typical of applications involving such techniques are; adaptive stock control systems, PERT and PERT COST, linear programming, forecasting, sensitivity analyses, model building, and simulations of all types.

Integration

The basic aim of an integrated system is easily stated. That is, the d.p. system takes account of all the implications of a transaction in one pass of the data. Unfortunately, this is easier to state than to achieve. Although no company would claim to have a fully integrated d.p. system, various facets of systems have been integrated with advantage. For example, the integration of customer order handling, stock control, invoicing and sales ledger can bring substantial benefits. These are, for instance, avoidance of despatching goods to customers with bad credit records, back orders dealt with more rationally, and stock control and re-ordering kept more in tune with incoming orders.

Data-base

A data-base may be simply described as the records and information which are accessible within the d.p. system.

Records have always existed but a well designed d.p. system enables the records to be held more comprehensively, permits searching interrogations (not necessarily on a real-time basis), shows the relationships between records and, in general, permits management to be better informed provided that management is aware of the potentialities of the d.p. system and the information that is available for the asking. This is undoubtedly a benefit on occasions but quantification in this area is most difficult. It will be necessary for each manager to consider the types of interrogation he will require, the use to which he will put the information supplied, and to provide some quantitative measure that can be used as a crude form of assessment.

This last factor may not be as nebulous as it sounds, for each manager has a more or less defined area of responsibility, facets of which are likely to be measurable.

Summary of benefits assessment

Not all of the above benefits apply to every application and it is unhesitatingly conceded that quantification in some of the areas is possible only very approximately. However, it is considered that a very real attempt should be made to spell out the benefits expected, in terms of ratios, percentages, volumes, timings, and values, not only for the purpose of the initial appraisal but also to provide control factors for the post-installation audit of benefits actually gained compared with expectations.

8.5   Taxation implications

The aim of this section is to indicate the main taxation implications involved in the investment appraisal and makes no claim to deal with taxation intricacies.

Taxation must be considered in the appraisal because it has an effect on the organisation's cash flow. When a computer is purchased it is possible to claim capital allowances of 80 per cent of cost in the first year and 25 per cent of the balance of cost in each of the subsequent years, calculated on the reducing balance method. In development areas a 100 per cent write-off is allowed in the first year; this presupposes that enough profits are available to take advantage of the allowances.

In addition, if the operation of the d.p. system is expected to produce surpluses (profits) these will be taxed at the prevailing rate of corporation tax. All running costs of the system, including any lease and rental payments, are allowable business expenses.

The effects of tax advantages (tax savings through capital allowances) and tax disadvantages (tax payments on profit) are not felt immediately because of the nature of the tax system whereby taxes are paid at periods varying from 9 to 18 months after the end of the financial year. For the purposes of investment appraisal it is the cash flow position which is of importance, so it will be necessary to calculate not only the amount of tax to be paid but when it will be paid to the Collector of Taxes.

ORTREX LTD – CASE STUDY

Line No.		This year	Machine installation year	Installation year +1	+2	+3	+4	+5	+6	+7	+8
1	OPERATING COSTS Including DP salaries training conversion etc	−15,000	−35,000	−32,000	−36,000	−38,000	−38,000	−42,000	−36,000	−36,000	
2	BENEFITS Operational savings, clerical savings bureau charge savings.etc Managerial & control savings	−	+8,000	+35,000	+55,000	+60,000	+70,000	+75,000	+75,000	+80,000	
3	Reduction in debtors — optimistic .2 prob.		20,000	25,000	36,000	40,000	43,000	48,000	50,000	50,000	
	Reduction in stocks etc — most likely .6 prob.		16,000	22,000	29,000	34,000	40,000	42,000	45,000	45,000	
	pessimistic .2 prob.		10,000	18,000	21,000	24,000	26,000	30,000	35,000	38,000	
	(expected value)		+15,600	+21,800	+28,800	+33,200	+37,800	+40,800	+44,000	+44,600	
4	Operating surplus or deficiency	−15,000	−11,400	+24,800	+47,800	+55,200	+69,800	+73,800	+83,000	+88,600	
5	Equipment & accommodation costs	−12,000	−165,000	−	−25,000	−	−30,000	−	−	−	
6	Net cash flows (before taxation implications)	−27,000	−176,400	+24,800	+22,800	+55,200	+39,800	+73,800	+83,000	+88,600	

Taxation implications										(Balance of allowances)
For investment of										
Capital allowances — 12,000		9,600	600	450	337	254	189	142	107	321
165,000			132,000	8,250	6,187	4,640	3,481	2,610	1,958	5,874
25,000					20,000	1,250	937	703	527	1,583
30,000							24,000	1,500	1,125	3,375
7 Total capital allowances		9,600	132,600	8,700	26,524	6,144	28,607	4,955	3,717	11,153
8 Tax flows due to capital allowances		+3,840	+53,040	+3,480	+10,610	+2,458	+11,443	+1,982	+1,487	+4,461
9 Tax flows due to operating surplus or deficiency		+6,000	+4,560	−9,920	−19,120	−22,080	−27,920	−29,520	−33,200	−35,440
10 Net tax effects		+9,840	+57,600	−6,440	−8,510	−19,622	−16,477	−27,538	−31,713	−30,979
11 Net cash flow after tax effects	−27,000	−166,560	+82,400	+16,360	+46,690	+20,178	+57,323	+55,462	+56,887	−30,979
12 Discount factors @ 10%	1.0	.909	.826	.751	.683	.621	.564	.513	.466	.424
13 Discounted net cash flow	−27,000	−151,403	+68,062	+12,286	+31,889	+12,530	+32,330	+28,452	+26,509	−13,135

∴ NPV = +£20,520

Notes:
Line 4 = 1 + 2 + 3
Line 6 = 4 + 5
Line 8 = 40% of line 7
Line 9 = 40% of line 4 (with 1 year lag)
Line 10 = 8 + 9
Line 11 = 6 + 10
Line 13 = 12 × 11

− = cash outflow
+ = cash inflow

FIG. 8.2 Case study—data processing system investment appraisal

8.6 Case study—data processing system investment appraisal

Having established and estimated the costs, values of benefits, and the taxation implications, the net cash flows in each period can be ascertained and the DCF calculations made.

As an illustration consider the following, much simplified, case study of a typical appraisal.

ORTREX LIMITED is a medium sized pharmaceutical company contemplating the acquisition of a computer and the installation of a d.p. system. A study team, consisting of a consultant and three members of staff, has carried out a comprehensive survey of the organisation.

The study has covered sales order handling, invoicing, sales ledger, stock control, purchasing and the provision of management information at each stage. The progressive implementation of the scheme involves additional equipment (line 5 of Fig. 8.2) and a rundown of clerical staff over the period of implementation (line 2 of Fig. 8.2). The amount and timings of all costs have been estimated (lines 1 and 5 of Fig. 8.2). It has been decided that the system should be appraised over 7 years and at the end of this period it is expected that the equipment will have no residual value.

The taxation situation is: corporation tax rate 40 per cent, capital allowances 80 per cent of cost in the first year and 25 per cent per annum on the reducing balance thereafter. Sufficient profits are available to take advantage of any capital allowances and a 1 year lag for taxation cash flows has been assumed. Using these assumptions the taxation consequences have been calculated (lines 7, 8, 9 and 10 of Fig. 8.2).

The benefits of the proposed system have been estimated by the study team, line management, and the Financial Director (lines 2 and 3 of Fig. 8.2).

Some of the savings are readily ascertainable, e.g. the savings of fees charged by a local bureaux for a monthly statistical job, which will, in future, be carried out by Ortrex's own computer. These are termed operational savings (line 2 of Fig. 8.2). The other savings, termed managerial and control savings, are considered to be less certain so the study team, in conjunction with the line management involved, have estimated subjective probabilities for three possible levels, *viz.* optimistic, most likely and pessimistic. The expected values (probability of outcome × value of outcome) have been calculated for these benefits (line 3 of Fig. 8.2).

The Financial Director considers that the most appropriate discount rate to use is 10 per cent.

The full details of the appraisal are set out in Fig. 8.2.

The NPV of +£20,520 indicates that the proposed d.p. system is worthwhile and, if management are satisfied that the estimates, assumptions, and probabilities incorporated in the analysis are reasonable, then the investment should be initiated.

It should be noted that although the figures used are quite arbitrary they probably reflect the typical situation in that tangible cost savings are not sufficient to make the project worthwhile and some assessment of intangible benefits is necessary.

8.7 Leasing

At this point readers may wonder why leasing has not been mentioned as it is a popular method of acquiring substantial assets such as computers.

Leasing is a method of financing whereby the title to the goods remains permanently vested in the lessor. The effect of this is that the lessee forgoes capital allowances but is able to treat the whole of the leasing charge as revenue expenditure and offset the charges against Corporation Tax. Although the legal position of leasing differs from normal borrowing, for example, leasing commitments are not normally shown on the balance sheet, leasing is in its effect a form of implicit borrowing whereby the lessee is committed to a series of future payments. These payments include the outright purchase price, interest and financing charges.

Although the literature of leasing companies suggests substantial savings and advantages of leasing compared with outright purchase, the analysis of the two propositions is somewhat complex and a number of steps are necessary.

1 First establish whether the acquisition is worthwhile to the organisation, namely, is the project profitable in itself; does it meet the required rate of return? This is done as outlined in the ORTREX case study above. The reason for this is that there are two decisions involved in the appraisal process, an investment decision and a financing decision, they should be kept separate otherwise nonsensical results may occur. The source of funds should not affect the investment decision but the cost of various sources of funds does affect the financing decision.

2 Assuming acquisition has been decided upon, calculate the incremental cash flow effects of the purchasing alternative compared with the best leasing plan.

For example, assume it has been already decided to acquire an asset costing £100,000. The choice is between outright purchase and the best leasing plan, which is, say, 25 per cent per annum for 5 years. For simplicity at this stage taxation and all other considerations are ignored.

		Cash flows in years				
		0	1	2	3	4
A	Purchase	−100,000	—	—	—	—
B	Lease	−25,000	−25,000	−25,000	−25,000	−25,000
C	Incremental cash flows A−B	−75,000	+25,000	+25,000	+25,000	+25,000

The incremental cash flows of the notional purchasing project are the savings that will be gained by purchasing rather than leasing.

3 The NPV of this notional project should be calculated using the organisation's opportunity cost of capital or the target rate of return for risk-free projects. The notional project being considered is for practical purposes virtually risk-free as the purchase price is known and the lease payments are legally fixed by the leasing agreement. (The risk characteristics involved in the *investment decision* are quite separate and should be considered at that stage. At present the *financing decision* is being considered.)

For example if it is assumed that the target rate of return for risk-free projects is 10 per cent, the NPV of the incremental cash flows calculated above is as follows.

	Year				
	0	1	2	3	4
Incremental cash flows	−75,000	+25,000	+25,000	+25,000	+25,000
Discount Factors @ 10 per cent	1·0	0·909	0·826	0·751	0·683
Discounted values	−75,000	+22,725	+20,650	+18,775	+17,075

$$NPV = +£4,225$$

4 If the NPV is positive at the target rate of return for risk-free investments then this means that the purchase alternative is preferable. To see that this is correct, assume that the leasing payments are increased by £10,000 per annum in the above example. The incremental cash flows would then be:

	Year				
	0	1	2	3	4
Incremental cash flows	−65,000	+35,000	+35,000	+35,000	+35,000

and the NPV would be +£45,915 making the purchase alternative even more desirable as it would obviously be if leasing payments increased.

The basic steps in the lease/purchase decision are given, but to illustrate a more realistic situation consider the following case which is a continuation of the ORTREX Limited case study in Section 8.6.

8.8 Case study—lease versus purchase decision

The management of ORTREX LIMITED (see previous case study Section 8.6) have decided to acquire a computer and install a d.p. system but wish to examine various financing alternatives. After considerable investigation the Financial Director has estimated that the best alternative to purchasing is a plan put forward by LEESIT LIMITED which provides for leasing payments at the rate of 25 per cent per annum over 5 years, 30 per cent over 4 years and

Line No.		This year	Machine installation year	Installation year +1	+2	+3	+4	+5	+6	+7	+8
	Assumptions 25% pa 5 yr / 30% pa 4 yr / 35% pa 3 yr										
	Equipment costs (From line 5 Figure 8.2)	12,000	165,000		25,000		30,000				
	Lease payments — Investment / Term										
	12,000 — 5 yrs	3,000	3,000	3,000	3,000	3,000					
	165,000 — 5 yrs	–	41,250	41,250	41,250	41,250	41,250				
	25,000 — 5 yrs				6,250	6,250	6,250	6,250	6,250		
	30,000 — 4 yrs						9,000	9,000	9,000	9,000	
1	Lease cash flows	−3,000	−44,250	−44,250	−50,500	−50,500	−56,500	−15,250	−15,250	−9,000	
2	Tax savings		+1,200	+17,700	+17,700	+20,200	+20,200	+22,600	+6,100	+6,100	+3,600
3	Net cash flow effect of leasing	−3,000	−43,050	−26,550	−32,800	−30,300	−36,300	+7,350	−9,150	−2,900	+3,600
4	Net cash flow effect of purchasing	−12,000	−161,160	+53,040	−21,520	+10,610	−27,542	+11,443	+1,982	+1,487	+4,461
5	Incremental purchasing "project" cash flows	−9,000	−118,110	+79,590	+11,280	+40,910	+8,758	+4,093	+11,132	+4,387	+861
6	Discount factors @ 8%	1.0	.926	.857	.794	.735	.681	.630	.583	.540	.500
7	Discounted incremental purchasing project cash flows	−9,000	−109,370	+68,209	+8,956	+30,069	+5,964	+2,579	+6,490	+2,369	+430

∴ NPV = +£6,696

Notes:
Line 2 = 40% line 1 (with 1 yr lags)
Line 3 = line 1 + line 2
Line 4 = line 5 + line 8 (both from Figure 8.2)   i.e. Purchasing + capital allowance cash flows cash flows
Line 5 = line 4 − line 3
Line 7 = line 6 × line 5

FIG. 8.3   Lease/purchase case study

35 per cent per annum over 3 years. Leasing payments normally consist of payments over a primary period (say 25 per cent for 5 years) then a nominal rate over a secondary period (say 1 per cent for 3 years). For simplicity the secondary period has been ignored. It has been decided to spread the leasing payments over as long a period as possible within the 7 year appraisal period considered. The summary of the lease cash flows is given in line 1 of Fig. 8.3. The tax savings due to the lease payments, with the appropriate one year lags, are given in line 3 of Fig. 8.3.

The net cash flow effect of purchasing, that is the purchasing cash outflows less the taxation saved through capital allowances is brought forward from Fig. 8.2.

The Financial Director estimates that an appropriate discount rate to use is 8 per cent.

The analysis of the lease/purchase decision is set out in Fig. 8.3.

The analysis shows that at an 8 per cent discount rate the NPV of the notional purchasing/lease project is +£6,696 making purchase clearly preferable in this instance.

8.9 Financial appraisal after installation

Once the decision has been taken to install a d.p. system it is necessary to give detailed consideration to the methods by which control will be exercised. Data processing is no different from any other commercial project in that success or failure is, in general, a reflection of the quality of management. The fact of a d.p. system being installed must be taken to mean that over-all profitability was assumed or expected at the start. The main aim of control procedures is to ensure that this planned profitability is not eroded. This erosion can be due to many causes, some of which are as follows:

1 Unplanned increases in d.p. staff and equipment.
2 Unplanned increases in operating costs.
3 Projects not being implemented to schedule.
4 Expected clerical staff reductions not achieved.
5 Unexpected difficulties in systems analysis, programming, acceptance by customers or employees.
6 Additional requirements externally or internally imposed, e.g. new government requirements on the amount of disclosure necessary, fundamental changes in pricing structures.
7 Anticipated benefits not realised, e.g. cycle time of production not reduced, stock/debtors ratios static.

Management's task is therefore to attempt to keep within the original targets (or to improve them) or, where modifications are necessary, to show the effects of modifications and the resulting new plans.

Control cycle

Whatever level of control is being considered—strategic, tactical or operational, the elements of the control cycle should be observed.

Briefly these elements are:

1 Establishment of control data in the form of an initial plan, budget or standard. This may be done on the basis of judgment, experience, observation, calculation or work measurement.
2 The appropriate plan, budget or standard is agreed with the persons to be controlled and, after agreement, is implemented accordingly.
3 Details of actual performance are recorded. These may be times taken, work completed, money spent, stationery used, etc.
4 Differences between the actual and planned performance are determined and possible causes established.
5 Action is taken to rectify each significant variance encountered by more supervision, revised methods, more training, better quality staff or the incorporation of incentives.

The detail in the plan and the review period will vary according to the level involved.

An outline of possible relationships between strategic, tactical, and operational planning and control, and of typical review periods is given in Fig. 8.4.

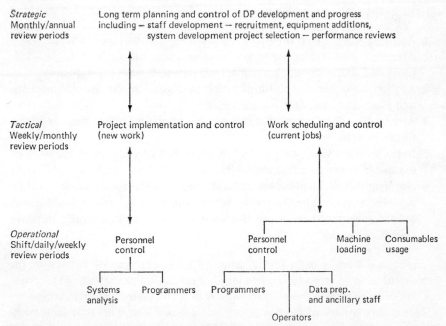

FIG. 8.4   Outline of planning and control of data processing department

Essentially the problem of planning and control resolves itself into three elements—what is to be done?—how is it to be done?—how well are targets met?

Although every aspect of data processing operations affects over-all profitability in one way or other, some aspects are undoubtedly of major financial significance. These are:

1 Project selection.
2 Project control.
3 Performance appraisal.

8.10   Project selection

However well the data processing department is run and however 'advanced' the equipment, if the computer is employed in the wrong projects or applications, over-all profitability is hardly likely to be achieved. A simple criterion is that all applications should be implemented which achieve a target rate of return. The problem remains; how can such applications be recognised? Many organisations using computers have virtually had the project selection problem answered for them because of the presence of some particular intractable, large scale job. An example of this is the massive billing operation carried out by the various gas and electricity boards.

Without such an obvious application a number of factors could be considered in the selection process.

1 Areas of work which involve large scale repetitive clerical operations.
2 Areas of work where large amounts of information have to be filed, processed and accessed, particularly if repeated access is necessary.
3 Any operations and procedures which involve excessive manual/mechanised calculations and/or reproduction.
4 Areas of work where staff shortages are apparent, either now or in the future.
5 Areas where savings are possible by increased speed, greater accuracy or the use of more scientific methods.
6 Applications which assist the main stream activities (production, marketing, distribution, stockholding, purchasing etc.) to reduce cycle times, reduce inventories or waste, increase turnover and generally improve operating ratios.

There seems to be little formal attempt to assess priority ratings in the implementation of projects, but one large organisation has attempted to assess the sequence of implementation by means of a calculated priority rating.

This rating is derived from a points scale associated with four factors, as follows:

1 *Interdependence with other sections of work*   *Points*
  Holds up work in 1 section   2
  Holds up work in 2 sections   4
  Holds up work in more than 2 sections   6
  Depends on development in other sections   −1
2 *Operations savings, i.e. clerical savings, etc.*   *Points*
  Breakeven in 1 year or less from implementation   8
  Breakeven in 2 years or less from implementation   6
  Breakeven in 3 years or less from implementation   4
  Breakeven in 4 years or less from implementation   2
  Breakeven in 5th year or later   1
3 *Less tangible savings, i.e. better management control, etc.*   *Points*
  Big and definite   4
  Small and definite   3
  Big and indefinite   2
  Small and indefinite   1
4 *Required to round off controls*   *Points*
  Improves controls in up to 2 other sections   1
  Improves controls in up to 3 or more sections   2

From an assessment of the factors above the relative priorities for implementation can be established, albeit in broad terms. However, it should be noted that all the priority rating calculated above provides is a guide to the sequence of implementation. Detailed financial appraisals as discussed in previous sections of this chapter must still be carried out.

8.11 Control and standards—general considerations

The planning and control of new project implementation has certain common features with the operational control of existing jobs.

It is in these areas that forms of budgetary control can be used effectively. Budgets are resource plans, that is, what is planned to attain, expressed in financial terms.

It is important to realise that the resource plans, expressed in numbers of people, equipment, time, and quantities, are the budgeted items and *not* the financial figures. The financial representation is merely a very useful common denominator that relates diverse factors such as the number of system analysts employed on a project, the volume of printed output from the d.p. system, and the extra peripheral units required for expansion.

Because many of the elements of data processing expenditure are fixed for some time in the future, e.g. salaries, rentals, maintenance and many operating costs, there is little value in over-all and departmental budgetary control procedures. What is of importance in data processing is the effective utilisation of resources, particularly people. To be of real value control procedures, including budgetary control, must be on a functional or output basis. This means that there must be recognition that the data processing department is engaged in investigating and implementing new projects, and operating existing systems. Plans should be made, resources allocated, and comparisons made in relation to these tasks. The over-all costs of the data processing department will therefore be made up of the individual task costs, and the real control will occur over the resources used within each of the functional areas and not in some over-all global fashion.

To plan and control effectively it will be apparent that there must be some form of standards of performance showing times, volumes, efficiencies, and capacities of all activities within the data processing orbit.

Methods and performance standards

The establishment of standards of procedure, methods and performance is a very detailed technical matter and is not the accountant's function. The establishment of detailed and comprehensive standards is the task of the data processing manager and his staff.

If the financial appraisal of data processing activities is the accountant's responsibility it behoves him to ensure that some attempt at least is made to establish, publish, and continually refine methods and performance standards. If this is not done, it is directly analogous to attempting to superimpose a standard costing system on a manufacturing process where no works study or work measurement has taken place.

A data processing standards manual should therefore be published. This will act as a means of communication and as a basis for comparison of actual results. Typically, such a manual would contain sections on:

1 Systems analysis standards.
2 Programming standards.
3 Operating standards.
4 Performance standards.

A brief outline of typical contents of these sections is given below but readers who wish to pursue the subject in greater depth, are advised to consult the manufacturer's literature or one of the texts on the subject [14].

Systems analysis standards

1 Standards of output layouts and design, and so on.
2 Flow-charting symbols and conventions to be adopted.
3 Sequence of analysis, documentation and authorisation required at each stage.
4 Documentation standards, cross referencing, indexing, etc.
5 Glossary of data processing and organisation terminology.

Programming standards

1 Programming sequence and logical analysis—flow charting, coding etc.
2 Test data preparation
3 Compilation and/or assembly procedures.
4 Testing procedures.
5 Documentation standards.
6 Operating instruction standards.
7 Program organisation—restart points, error routines, etc.
8 Revision and amendment procedures.

Operating standards

1 Shift arrangements and responsibilities.
2 Time logging procedures.
3 Control functions.
4 Machine operating procedures—set up, file changes, take down.
5 Emergency procedures.
6 Reordering and control procedures for stationery, consumables, etc.
7 File and program library operation—issue, storage, usage records.

Performance standards

From the viewpoint of the accountant, this section of the Standards Manual is of most relevance as the details contained provide the basis for many important areas of control, *viz.* project control, budgetary and cost control, scheduling and machine loading.

It is important to realise that performance standards reflect the methods and procedure standards outlined previously.

Performance standards may be built up from past experience and past time recordings but inevitably judgements play a part, particularly with regard to programming and systems analysis time standards. Although some areas contain broad approximations it is vital that some initial estimate is made, and documented, and progressively refined as experience grows.

Typical of performance standards are the following:

1 Program run time standards based on input volumes, complexity, and print volumes.
2 Compilation time standards.
3 Operator time standards.
4 Data preparation and coding time standards.
5 Systems analysis time standards—often broad time bands for systems investigation, systems design, and specification writing based on such factors as complexity, number of functions, number of interviews, degree of standardisation existing, etc.

6 Programming time standards—the basic factors influencing programming time are program size and complexity.

In the early days of an installation performance standards are likely to be rudimentary. Nevertheless they should be initiated at the outset, and expanded and amended as experience grows. Only in this way can planning and control be made more effective.

8.12 Project control

Excluding hardware costs, most of the money spent on data processing is probably incurred in the development and implementation of new projects. It is of prime importance for this area of data processing activity to be carefully planned and closely controlled, not only for the expenditures incurred but for the benefits foregone by not having the system implemented at the earliest possible time. An incidental benefit from close project control is the data on actual performance that can be used to refine the Performance Standards discussed above, and this may be of some value in personnel assessment.

Numerous refinements in project control are possible but the steps given below provide a basis for a workmanlike system.

1 All projects should have a unique reference number.

2 Each project should be subdivided into stages which correspond to the main areas of work involved. Examples of typical subdivisions are:

Feasibility study.
Systems investigation.
Systems design.
Program design.
Program writing and testing.
Systems implementation.

3 For each subdivision, estimates should be made of the number of personnel required, the time they should take, and computer time where necessary. It is essential for estimates to be made for each part of the project, a single global estimate for the whole project is virtually useless as a control device. The personnel to be involved in the project should be involved in the estimation process and must be aware of the final agreed figure.

4 Weekly, each staff member must record the time spent on any stage of the project. It is necessary to have various alternative codes for time booking, such as program maintenance, training, and travelling, so that a detailed and meaningful analysis of time spent is possible.

5 Weekly, as well as their personal time record, each member of staff (systems analysts, programmers), or section leader if a small team is engaged upon a segment, should make an estimate of the percentage completion of the particular phase being undertaken. The estimate of percentage completion can be used to monitor real progress and not merely the passing of time, indicate revised completion dates, and to pinpoint areas where serious delays may occur.

6 Any expenditure—excluding staff salaries—and computer time used for testing should be booked against the appropriate segment of the project.

7 Based on the original project segment estimates, the actual times taken, percentage completion estimates, expenditures, and computer time used, various weekly/monthly/quarterly/annual reports can be produced. These reports provide control and historical information for project leaders and data processing management.

Typical of such reports are the following.

Project time analysis

This report gives details of time estimates, start and estimated completion dates, time spent by staff and supervision, any revisions to completion dates necessary, amounts of schedule slippage expressed in hours. This analysis can be for the project as a whole or for individual phases of a project.

Phase progress reports

This report is for control at the individual level and shows: total estimated time, start date, cumulative and time spent in current period for each individual staff member, the percentage completion, revised completion date and variance between this date and original estimate.

Manpower load report

This report gives details of every employee by project phase showing; work allocations, percentage completion of tasks, hours to completion (original estimate and revisions), and the calculated date of completion of each project phase.

Cost analysis

This report converts into £p the previous analyses and progress reports so as to provide an up-to-date comparison of budget, expenditure to date, and projected expenditure to completion. It is worth repeating that the real control lies in the underlying time and progress details, the cost analysis is merely a translation of this data into money terms.

As an illustration of some of the features of project control outlined above consider Figs 8.5, 8.6 and 8.7. Fig. 8.5 shows the project phases, the codes, and the original estimates. Fig. 8.6 shows the time sheets of the two system analysts at the end of the third week of the systems investigation.

From the details contained in Figs 8.5 and 8.6 each of the reports can be prepared. To illustrate a typical presentation the Phase Progress Report is shown in Fig. 8.7. This particular report can be used as the basis of monitoring progress at the individual level and provides a basis for decisions on the dispositions of personnel. For example, in project DP 2357-SI in Fig. 8.7 it is apparent that to achieve the original target date, $3\frac{1}{3}$ (100/30) additional man-weeks are required so that a possible decision would be to draft another systems analyst into the project to help White and Grey.

Project: Credit control — home industrial sales No DP2357				Start Date	10.1.72
Phase	Code	Estimated man hours	Estimated computer hours	No. of personnel	Target completion date*
Systems investigation	DP2357-SI	360	—	2	18.2.72
Systems design	DP2357-SD	240	—	2	17.3.72
Program design	DP2357-PD	120	—	1	14.4.72
Program writing	DP2357-PW	360	20	3	12.5.72
Systems implementation	DP2357-IM	120	10	2	26.5.72

*Based on net 30 hr/week/person

FIG. 8.5 Project control—basic data

Clearly most of the work associated with project control can be handled by the computer and a number of computer packages are available for this purpose. A comprehensive example is the package being marketed in this country by Hoskyns [15].

8.13 Performance appraisal

There is a need to formally appraise the over-all effectiveness of the d.p. system and to consider future developments in terms of equipment, systems and personnel.

A typical review period for this appraisal would be annual. It is essentially an attempt to learn from experience and should not be an excuse for a high-level mud-slinging contest. The normal participants in such an appraisal

Timesheet			W/E:- 28.1.72
Name: B. White			Clock No: 98352
Project/code	Hours	% Completion	Comments
DP2357-SI	27	40	
DP2355-IM	5	100	Problem on Inventory control implementation at Bristol Factory
*GA 530	8		
Total	40		
Ordinary time:- 37 hrs Overtime:- 3 hrs			

*Travelling

Timesheet			W/E:- 28.1.72
Name: R. Grey			Clock No: 90321
Project/code	Hours	% Completion	Comments
DP2357-SI	30	40	
GA620	7	—	In service training on system standards
Total	37		
Ordinary time:- 37 hrs Overtime:- Nil			

FIG. 8.6   Project control—time sheets

would be the data processing manager, chief systems analyst, chief programmer, managers from user departments and a member of top management. It may be useful to include an impartial outsider, such as an experienced data processing consultant.

The appraisal should be wide-ranging, and typical of the areas to be thoroughly probed are the following.

Personnel and organisation

Review of the organisation of data processing department.

PHASE PROGRESS REPORT

W/E 28.1.72

Project: Credit control — home industrial sales

Project/code	Phase	Name	Hours B/F	Hours this week	Cum hours	% completion	Estimated hours		Target date		Schedule hours adv/slippage
							Original	Revised	Original	Revised	
DP2357 Systems investigation		B. White	68	27	95	40					
"	"	R. Grey	60	30	90	40					
			128	57	185		360	460	18.2.72	1.3.72	−100

FIG. 8.7 Project control—sample report

Degree of non-data processing management participation.
Recruitment, staff turnover, promotions and gradings.
Training undertaken during year.
Future plans and policies in these areas.

Applications implemented

Have objectives and deadlines been met? Have expected benefits in terms of
   clerical savings, control savings etc. been realised?
Are user departments satisfied with service?
Are there any defects in existing applications?
Future plans and policies in these areas.

Controls and standards

What has been progress on budgets/cost control/project control?
What have been the computer utilisation ratios?
Review of progress on standards (systems analysis, programming, operating
   and documentation).
Performance of control section, coding and data preparation.
Auditor's report.
Future plans and policies in these areas.

Equipment

Suitability of main-frame, peripherals, data conversion equipment and any
   other hardware.
Maintenance performance and down-time statistios.
Future plans and policies in these areas.

Although many of the above items are not immediately financial they all
contribute to the situation being reviewed. That is to say, is the d.p. system
efficient, appropriate, capable of development and above all, is it cost/benefit
effective?

Chapter 9 Auditing and Control of Data Processing Systems

9.1 Accounting and data processing systems

All accountants, whether acting as internal or external auditors, company secretaries, financial or management accountants, are likely to be faced either now or in the future with audit and control problems associated with d.p. systems.

The main problems, as always, are caused by people and not by the machines. Computers transfer, calculate and generally manipulate data with unprecedented accuracy, yet errors and frauds still occur. There is a tendency to seize upon and embellish all stories of errors and mismanagement in any way associated with computers without any corresponding attention being given to the millions of transactions which are processed correctly day in and day out. Although some exaggerations have occurred it would be less than honest not to admit that not all computer systems are adequately controlled in the accounting sense. Why is this so?

This is basically due to inadequate attention to the control and auditing aspects of d.p. systems in the early planning stages. A considerable number of time-tested control methods used with clerical and mechanised systems are just as appropriate to d.p. systems.

There is a tendency to forget that the computer is but one part of an information system which encompasses many clerical functions both before and after the computer operations. These areas are potential sources of error and as such must be given as much attention as the computer system and computer programs.

In the scramble to develop d.p. systems over the past decade, too little attention has been paid to questions of profitability (discussed in Chapter 8) and to the control and audit aspects of d.p. systems. The principles of control are, of course, not only applicable to the obviously financial applications such as payroll, costing, and ledger work but are equally necessary for all facets of an organisation's systems.

As examples of frauds that have occurred consider the following brief cases:

1 A programmer working in an American bank increased his own overdraft limit from $2,000 to $200,000.
2 Invoices for non-existent goods from fake companies were settled through a computer-based accounting system. This will be immediately recognised as a classical type of fraud known and practised long before the advent of computers.
3 The unauthorised sale of spare computer time to outside users.
4 The unauthorised sale of computer printouts containing vital information to competitors.
5 The pirating of system specifications, flow charts and program details by data processing personnel, and their subsequent sale to rival organisations.

Unfortunately, only unsuccessful frauds can be investigated and clearly there must be others as yet undiscovered.

It would be unrealistic to imagine that a completely watertight system can be devised. Intelligent, determined men with the requisite technical skills who are employed by the organisation could, in time, beat any system of control. What is necessary, is to ensure that a series of interlocking checks and controls over personnel, systems and machines make the possibility of fraud extremely remote.

The reasons for data processing control procedures

Fortunately for the auditor a considerable proportion of the aims of data processing management coincide with the aims of the auditor. The data processing manager is concerned, inter alia, to ensure that

All data that is required to be processed *is* processed.
All data processed is identified correctly and dealt with accordingly.
Incorrect items of data are identified and dealt with either clerically or within the d.p. system according to the prescribed rules.
Correct data are not corrupted before, during or after computer processing.
Generally to ensure that the d.p. system is working in an efficient and effective manner.

To carry out the functions mentioned above it is necessary to consider in detail the controls and security checks that must be incorporated into a comprehensive system in order to safeguard the organisation, the users, and the people employed within the data processing department.

It is absolutely mandatory for all system controls to be systematic, well documented and publicised, and for management to ensure that they are adhered to. Indeed, one of the main changes in emphasis of the auditor in relation to d.p. systems, is to spend more time checking the existence, operation, and effectiveness of system's controls rather than detailed individual entry and item vouching, although the latter does not entirely disappear.

Paradoxically, most of the control procedures necessary with d.p. systems deal with people and their work and not with the operations of computers. Consequently most of the control features to be described deal with matters outside the direct computer environment but which, nevertheless, have important effects on the security and efficiency of the whole d.p. system of which the computer is the central part.

In general, the framework of over-all control procedures must be explicitly considered when the data processing department is first established. The special individual controls necessary for each new application or job incorporated into the d.p. system, must be designed within this over-all control framework. There are thus two levels of control: the general framework for the department, and the particular controls for each application. All control procedures must be considered at the planning and design stages, they cannot be successfully grafted on to existing organisations and existing systems.

Control procedures are of some importance with clerical systems but they become vitally significant with d.p. systems. There are a number of reasons for this:

1 The general complexity and size of d.p. systems.
2 The partial or complete breakdown of the normal personal, functional and departmental divisions of responsibility, and the consequent telescoping of functions into the data processing department.
3 The partial or complete loss of traditional audit trails owing to the integration of clerical procedures into linked suites of computer programs where there may be little or no printed intermediate output.
4 The problems associated with the invisibility of processing and recording on magnetic storage media such as tapes, disks and drums.
5 The often massive increase in paper flow from and to one department of the organisation whereas previously paper work travelled in smaller batches to many more destinations.
6 The loss of personal scrutiny and checking inherent in many clerical systems when work and documents are passed from department to department that each carry out some facet of the organisation. In many d.p. systems the only individual scrutiny may be during data conversion which is not intended in any way to be a vetting operation.
7 The general unfamiliarity of non-data processing personnel with the system—many people only see a tiny link in the chain and may never see the end product, or worse, may not know what the system is supposed to produce.

To overcome the problems associated with the above points numerous controls are necessary and these will be considered under three headings:

1 ORGANISATIONAL CONTROLS—general administrative controls over the organisation, division of duties and responsibilities in the data processing department. These controls will affect, in various degrees, all work carried out by the data processing department and are part of the framework of control within which each new application is placed.

2 DEVELOPMENT CONTROLS—general controls to ensure that all new systems being designed adhere to rigorous standards of documentation and procedure so that essential stages in the design, programming and testing of systems are not skimped or omitted. Together with the organisational controls mentioned above, development controls affect all new applications being designed.

3 PROCEDURAL AND OPERATING CONTROLS—these controls include clerical controls, both external to and within the data processing department, and computer checks embodied in individual programs. These controls will be specific to each application and may contain unique features although it is likely that the broad pattern of controls associated with each application will be similar.

9.2 Organisational controls

In more traditional systems where work and documents are passed from person to person, department to department or function to function, divisions of responsibility are, to a large extent, automatic.

With d.p. systems all the work on a particular application may be carried out within the data processing department and thus the traditional department to department divisions of responsibility may be inapplicable. Because of this, it is necessary to replace the usual departmental/functional divisions of responsibility by divisions within the data processing department itself. This procedure is necessary for exactly the same reasons that adequate divisions of responsibility have been insisted on by auditors for generations, namely that if no one person handles a job from beginning to end fraud is not possible without collusion, and, if the job is subdivided, controls and checks can be more naturally introduced to ensure accuracy and adherence to procedures.

Clearly, the normal divisions of responsibilities, controls and segregation of duties still apply to all departments outside the data processing orbit but within this area a typical segregation of duties in a medium sized installation could be as shown in Fig. 9.1.

The work and responsibilities associated with each of the main areas shown in Fig. 9.1 are described below.

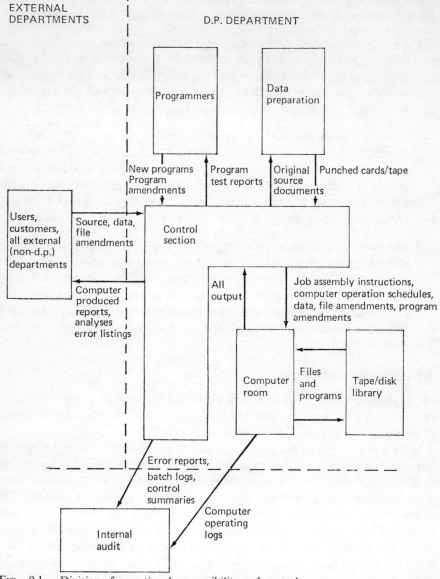

FIG. 9.1 Division of operational responsibility and control

Control section

This section is the hub of the control network and generally acts as a buffer between the rest of the data processing department, external user departments, and the actual computer room. From an operational viewpoint this section is the most important and this importance should be reflected in the quality and status of the staff. The physical location and layout of this section should be given careful consideration for, quite apart from specific control problems, the section will have a considerable paper handling problem dealing with the inflows of data and outflows of computer produced reports.

Specific areas of responsibility within the control section can be identified as follows:

1 Receipt of source documents containing original transaction data.

2 Checking that appropriate batch totals and batch numbers are attached to batches of source documents where it has been decided that these will be produced by departments external to the data processing department.

3 Control of movements of data batches to and from the data preparation section.

4 The provision of agreed operating instructions for each job to the computer operators, and the specification of file and program requirements to the tape/disk librarian.

5 The receipt and control of all amendments to standing file data. This type of input is of a fundamentally different character to transaction data such as hours worked, parts issued, goods despatched, etc. File amendments could involve relatively trivial changes such as a change of address or PAYE code or they could be more fundamental. Examples of such changes are, alterations in discount terms, credit limits or prices, reclassification of material categories, changes in the stored sequence of production processes for a particular product, etc.

Each amendment should be on the prescribed form which must specify the transaction code and the exact nature of the file amendment. Each type of amendment should have specified level of authorisation which should be appropriate to the possible consequences of the amendment.

For example, the signature of a supervisor in the Personnel department is likely to be sufficient for a routine change of address of an employee, whereas a change in discount terms to a major customer would probably require authorisation from the Sales Director. The transaction codes for amendments, the types of amendments possible, and the appropriate level of authorisation for each amendment type must be included in the systems design.

The foregoing items give the main areas of responsibility within the control section but because of the extreme importance of this section a number of important general safeguards should be observed.

1 Control section staff should have no other duties in the data processing department.

2 Apart from Control Section staff, nobody in the data processing department should be allowed to alter input data in any way or to make adjustment to batch control totals.

3 Control Section staff, or indeed any other data processing staff, should not have access to any clerically maintained records external to the data processing department, e.g. records of control totals of batches of source

documents sent by an external department to the data processing department.

4 Because of the potential importance of amendments to standing file data very careful control of the amendment procedure is necessary. In particular, master file changes should be initiated from within the data processing department only in exceptional cases, and then only after a prescribed authenticating procedure. In addition, a system of ensuring that file amendments have been correctly carried out is necessary. Clearly, no form of batching and totalling is appropriate to amendments which may or may not be numeric. The simplest system would seem to be a complete listing of amendments made in each run, this list showing, at a minimum, file information before amendment, file information after amendment and a cross reference to the original amendment form.

Computer room

Provided that adequate controls have been included in the system prior to the running of the job, the control aspects of the actual computer room are relatively straightforward and what is most important can be planned beforehand. The computer operators are responsible for running the jobs efficiently and according to schedule and the laid down operating instructions. Their work, which is a skilled task in its own right, involves the loading and unloading of card readers, tape units, disk drives and printers, running the correct programs and files on the computer, taking the specified actions in the event of error or programmed halts by the computer, and generally seeing that work flows through the computer room as quickly as possible.

The minimum controls necessary are as follows:

1 To ensure that all jobs have adequate, detailed operating instructions that are communicated to the operators in a standard format. All jobs must be run strictly in accordance with the prescribed instructions and where some divergence is necessary, because of unforeseen circumstances, this should be noted in the operating log.

2 The basic details of jobs run (files and programs used, times taken, etc.) should be logged. This computer log should preferably be maintained by the standard control programs of the computer and may appear on the console typewriter or may be recorded on backing storage for subsequent printout.

3 All interventions, whether routine or non-routine, and all direct console inputs should be programmed to appear in the operating log.

4 Only authorised operators should operate the computer and preferably these should be the only persons allowed in the computer room. In particular, programmers should NEVER be allowed to operate the machine when an operational job is being run.

5 Wherever the size of installation permits there should be two operators on duty and there should be rotation of duties.

Control of files and program library

It is astonishing how, even in a modest sized installation, the number of files and programs grows. Because of the number of files and their importance it is necessary to make sure that there is a competent tape/disk librarian or, at the very least, that the storage of files and programs is the responsibility of a designated operator.

The librarian's basic functions are firstly, to ensure that tapes and disks are maintained in correct environmental conditions—these are prescribed by the manufacturer—and secondly, to issue and receive for storage all files, programs, and scratch tapes in accordance with the job assembly instructions. In addition the librarian should, as far as possible, ensure that the correct files and programs are used and that wanted files are not over-written. This is partly a programming and software responsibility, as numerous checks should be incorporated into both operational programs and software.

There are certain controls and safeguards appertaining to file control; these are as follows:

1 Where the size of the installation permits, the librarian should have no other duties and, whether he has other duties or not, he should not have access to any form of clerically maintained external records.
2 Standing procedures should be established for the reconstruction of files in the event of accidental destruction. Normally this means that transaction data, in the form of punched cards or punched paper tape, is stored until subsequent generations of the file have been proved correct.
3 There should be adequate fire and flood precautions including the regular practice of storing duplicate copies of critical files and *all* programs at a separate location. Some care should be taken in the choice of the alternative location to avoid the unfortunate situation which confronted a large Bristol firm during the floods in 1967. This firm had two computer installations in the Bristol area and made a practice of storing copies of vital files and programs at both the installations. Unfortunately, this very sound procedure was nullified to a considerable extent owing to both installations being flooded to a depth of several feet on the same day!

The over-all aim of these controls and of the normal library procedures is to ensure that the correct files are used with the appropriate programs, and that a file is maintained intact until it has been superseded, usually by two later generations of the file.

9.3   System development controls

The various stages in systems analysis, synthesis and implementation have been described from the systems analyst's viewpoint in the previous chapters so will not be repeated in this section.

The main point of control procedures is to ensure that the often lengthy and complex task of designing and implementing a computer system, proceeds according to plan, is comprehensively documented, that no vital steps have been omitted, that appropriate procedural controls and safeguards have been specified, and that an amendment procedure for documenting system changes has been laid down.

An invaluable aid in the procedures applicable to all systems within the organisation is the D.P. Standards Manual of the installation. This Standards Manual sets out the basic framework of approach, documentation, terminology, form design, flow charting procedures and symbols which should be followed by all systems analysts and programmers (see Section 8.11).

Apart from these over-all standards, there are specific stages in the system development process that must be closely scrutinised for the inclusion of controls. The following sections can serve as either a basis for the development of a comprehensive audit program, or as a basis for advice whilst the system is being developed. There are clear advantages in being involved in the planning stages of a d.p. system, and if accountants, in whatever professional capacity, wish to be identified with computer systems, then early involvement is mandatory.

9.4 Procedural and operating controls

Whilst the system is being developed, decisions will be made as to whether a particular situation or type of input will be dealt with by the computer program or manually. Whatever this decision, it is necessary to ensure that a plan exists to cope with every eventuality and the purpose of procedural controls is to specify these plans in detail.

Procedural controls are clerical, operating and programming controls, all of which must be specified precisely whilst the system is being developed. Their main over-all purpose is to make certain that correct data is processed according to the agreed system so as to produce the required outputs.

It is important to appreciate that any review of controls in a computer-based system must include a scrutiny of the data flow and control systems from the origin of data, through the data processing department and the computer room, to the users of the outputs produced.

Because of this necessity for a comprehensive study of the total information flow the procedural controls will be described in six categories as follows:

A	Input controls	$\begin{cases} \text{Clerical} \\ \text{Computer} \end{cases}$
B	Main process and file controls	$\begin{cases} \text{Clerical} \\ \text{Computer} \end{cases}$
C	Output controls	$\begin{cases} \text{Clerical} \\ \text{Computer} \end{cases}$

A   Input Controls

Clerical—These controls commence in the department originating or first handling the source data.

The controls vary, in detail, between applications and whether the data is standing data, i.e. information such as wage rates, standard costs, etc., that are destined to be placed on files for reasonably long periods, amendments to standing data, e.g. wage rate changes, discount changes, changes in credit limits, etc., or whether the data relates to normal day-to-day transactions, e.g. cheques received, stock movements, purchase invoices received.

Any addition or amendment to file data must be on a properly designed form with an authorisation level appropriate to the type of amendment.

The amendment form should have a unique number, and cross reference should be possible from the input amendment form to the output list of the amendments made produced by the computer. Copies of all amendment forms should be filed in the control section or in the user department until audit verification has taken place.

Transaction data is normally controlled by means of batch control totals established over numeric data. This might be quantity, weight, volume, £p, number of lines or documents, or some other relevant quantity. Such data should be batched, with only one type of document in the batch, given a batch number and a control total derived by the user department. Although it is less than ideal, it is occasionally necessary for this work to be done by the control section in the data processing department. If this is done the division of responsibility is reduced and no check is possible on items lost in transit between the user department and the Control Section. For similar reasons it is even less desirable for the computer to first establish batch control totals to check input, even though the establishment of various controls by the computer for the checking of inter-program transfers is both normal and desirable.

Data of all types has to be converted into punched cards or punched paper tape unless OCR or MICR is used. It is necessary to ensure that the Data Conversion department is properly organised and, apart from environmental and ergonomic considerations, there are a number of control factors to be considered. These include, separate punching and verification of all data, close progressing of the flow of batches from and to the control section, carefully defined procedures for error correction and for dealing with indecipherable data on source documents.

The handling of errors at any stage is the supreme test of a system. Most systems cope with the basic flow of correct items but may fall down on the treatment of rejected items or situations which differ markedly from normal. For example, few systems would fail to notice a batch total which did not agree but can they cope with the non-arrival of a complete batch?

Computer—Because of the invisibility and automatic processing of computer-held files it is vital to eliminate invalid and incorrect data as early as possible in the suite of programs so as to reduce the risks of corrupting files. This would, of course, be catastrophic for most systems. Because of this, the data vetting and editing program is invariably the first program run in any suite of programs. The input data should be subjected to an exhaustive scrutiny by the data vetting program and the following are typical of the checks which should be included.

1 There should be modulus-11 check digit verification on all relevant keys, e.g. account numbers, part numbers, etc.

Check digits are the digit or digits which are added to key numbers to make these self-checking by the computer. The most commonly used of the check digit systems [10—see Section 5.5] is that termed 'modulus-11'. The check digit is established once only and thereafter forms part of the code, and there are four steps in the process of calculating it:

Step 1   Multiply each digit in the code number by a weighting factor, the digit in the least significant position has a weight of 2, the next a weight of 3, and so on.

Step 2   Add together the products of these multiplications.

Step 3   Divide this sum by 11.

Step 4   Subtract the remainder of Step 3 from 11; the result is the check digit, unless the remainder is zero in which case the check digit is also zero.

Example—the code 45264 would be operated on as follows.

Step 1	CODE NUMBER	4	5	2	6	4
	WEIGHTS	6	5	4	3	2
	PRODUCTS	24	25	8	18	8

Step 2 $24 + 25 + 8 + 18 + 8 = 83$.

Step 3 $83 \div 11 = 7$ and 6 remainder.

Step 4   Check digit $= 11 - 6 = 5$, and therefore code number is written as 452645.

When subsequently the code number is to be checked for validity the check digit is given a weight of 1 and the computer follows steps 1, 2 and 3. If the remainder is zero the code number is correct. If not the code number is rejected as incorrect.

2 Format checks—these check that each field of the input data contains the appropriate type of information whether alphabetic or numeric.

3 There should be a series of checks to ensure that each input data item has a valid transaction code together with the required data fields. For instance, a cash receipt should have a transaction code and two data fields; an account number and an amount.

36	128937	231.16
Unique	Account Number	Amount
transaction	with Modulus-11	
code	check digit	

4 Where input should be in sequence, the sequence should be checked and any gaps in the series should be reported, for example, Goods Received Notes should be in sequence and every one accounted for.

5 Where appropriate, the previously prepared batch totals should be checked. In general, where there is disagreement in the batch total the batch should be identified and rejected by the computer. It is normal to print out all the items in a rejected batch as this is an aid to error location.

6 Where possible each field in the input data should be checked for feasibility. This would normally be done by comparing the input value against maximum and/or minimum values expected for that particular data item.

For example, the trade discount inserted by the Sales Department on an incoming order would be compared with an upper limit of discount for the particular class of customer. This type of check is important because it partially replaces the clerical scrutiny associated with manual systems.

7 Basic radix checks would also be made, e.g. not more than 24 hrs booked in any one day or more than 20 cwt in any ton, and so on.

Any input item which fails one or more of the above checks is rejected for some form of later clerical action. This is an important area and, since the clerical procedures for dealing with errors on input are similar to those associated with the main processing parts of the suite, the description of the safeguards is dealt with immediately below.

B   Main processing and file controls

Clerical—Provided that processing is proceeding according to plan and no errors are found by the programs, little clerical intervention is involved. However, it is necessary to institute clerical control procedures to cover the situations when errors are found on single data items or where batch totals do not agree or the contents of a suspense file is printed out.

When an error is discovered by program, enough information should be printed to enable a full clerical investigation to be carried out. In the case of a disagreement over a batch control total the whole batch would usually need to be printed. The main purpose of clerical systems dealing with errors is to progress the action taken to rectify the error and to re-input the offending item or batch, or to deal with the situation completely outside the computer.

Ideally, the computer should retain a suspense file containing details of errors found, data rejections and control total disagreements; and periodically the items not cleared should be reported by the machine. In this way no errors are overlooked but where a computer-based file is not practicable a similar suspense file or error log should be retained by the control section for the purpose of progressing errors.

Probably the simplest way is for the printout of the error to contain consecutive numbers for each error and the actual printout retained by the control section to serve as their log.

Clearly, whilst a system for progressing the work involved in error correction is necessary, what is even more desirable is to reduce the number of errors or eliminate them entirely.

Something which has been found to be of considerable value in this respect, particularly in the early days of any application, is an analysis of errors found. Typical of the headings in such an analysis would be: source of data item, type of error (for example, incorrect batch total, incorrect check digit, mispunching, program error, operator error), volume of errors, average time to re-input error, number of the same errors in last corresponding period.

Computer—The controls described in this section are those included in the operational programs and are not hardware controls such as parity checks and read-after-write checks built into the system by the manufacturer.

Some checks on input cannot be made at the original data vetting stage and can only be carried out during the main file updating run. An example of this is the checking of the existence of a master file record to match with an input data item. In addition, some more obscure error situations can only be found when the main file contents are compared with the particular transaction item. For instance, a proposed change in piece work rates to a permanent hourly paid worker, or the proposed change to a 20 per cent discount rating to a customer who is already on 20 per cent discount.

All data flowing through the computer system should be labelled sufficiently to identify its source until it is completely processed and found to be correct.

During processing, controls are necessary so that some check is possible on the functioning of the program, and this is usually done by maintaining various control accounts. These are basically of two types: firstly internal accounts that are used in the programs in order to ensure correct transmission of data from one processing run to another, and which are not printed out unless there is a discrepancy; secondly, external accounts that are always printed out, and which provide a vertification of clerically prepared totals. On occasions, external accounts are the prime source of totals and serve as a basis for final accounts.

All important cumulative items on each file should be reconciled in a brought forward/carried forward account form.

The following example shows an account which could be used to control a stock file, or more precisely, the values in a stock file. Quantities, weights etc. would need to be controlled in similar but separate control accounts.

Stock value control account
1 Value of stock at start of period.
2 PLUS value of receipts.
3 PLUS value of returns.
4 PLUS or MINUS value of price changes on goods already received.
5 MINUS value of issues.
6 PLUS or MINUS value of discrepancies from stock checks.
7 MINUS value of stock write-offs through breakage, pilferage and evaporation.
8 MINUS value of depreciation.
9 MINUS value of stock carried forward.

This type of account is needed to control all cumulative items in each file.

In addition to this, cross-balancing controls are required to prove the correctness of arithmetic, and these are identical in principle to any form of cross-casting used in manual systems. An example would be the accumulation of cross balancing controls for a budgetary control summary as shown in Fig. 9.2.

C   Output controls

Clerical—The main purposes of controls at this stage are to make certain

Type of expense	Dept A	Dept B		Dept Z	Totals	
Code Description						
100 Copper						
101 Bronze						
						Cross balancing controls
Totals						

Cross balancing controls

FIG. 9.2   Cross-balancing controls

that the appropriate user or user department receives the correct output without undue delay and that no unauthorised printing nor file accessing takes place.

Proper captions and identifying information on output reports aid correct distribution and, where appropriate, sequential numbering by the computer serves as an additional check. This last point is particularly important with error reports where the main priority must be to ensure that error conditions are rectified and where necessary re-input to the computer. The best safe-guards against unauthorised printing and accessing are those discussed in Section 9.2, Organisational Controls.

Computer—Although the computer cannot help with the distribution of the printed output, some controls can be incorporated to help correct distribution and to make the output more meaningful.

1 Limit checks—these program checks test that computer calculated values, based on transaction data and file information, fall within predetermined limits. For example, no persons' overtime payments should be more than 50 per cent of basic wage in any week. This situation may happen and may be correct but a note should be made for an entry in the wages exception report.

2 Any output other than the main production output of the system, such as payslips, invoices and so on, should contain the reasons for the output. Examples are exception or control total print-out, information request or computer-detected fault. Wherever appropriate, as in the case of an information request, a cross-reference should be made to the initiating department or user.

3 Output should always have meaningful captions, page numbers and dates.

Each type of report should have its own series of sequential numbering of pages and, where necessary, line numbers within pages.

9.5 Real-time or 'on-line' systems

The previous sections deal with the control aspects of batch processing systems which are still by far the most commonly encountered. There is, however, a growing number of real-time or on-line systems being installed.

These systems accentuate the control problems encountered with batch processing systems although most of the control principles already described are applicable to the newer systems.

There are four problem areas connected with real-time systems which pose additional control problems and, which make the early consideration of control features even more essential. These problem areas are as follows.

1 Input is generally not batched, therefore it is normal for the computer system to receive random input of diverse types.

2 There may be an even sketchier audit trail than with batch processing systems. This is because of the input and output methods which are used. For example, in an on-line production control system quantities produced may be keyed directly into a shop floor terminal without any form of documentation. Similarly, works instructions may be in the form of visual displays with no printed output of conventional form.

3 Real time systems tend to be larger and more complex and there is increased inter-relationships between sections of the system. This means that it could be possible for a direct input from a remote terminal to update not just one file but several.

4 Because of the inherent immediacy of response of real-time systems, faster action is possible.

Indeed, this is one of the undoubted potential benefits of such systems, but this facility is only of value with a fully controlled and accurate response and becomes a positive disadvantage if incorrect output responses, caused by incorrect input and/or programming, are given.

Generally, the more 'real-time' and immediate the system becomes the more emphasis should be given to the organisational and system controls previously described.

Because of the particular nature of the method of data input the problems of control of input procedures are even more pronounced than with conventional systems. With real-time systems there is immediate access into the data-base underlying the whole system, so stringent controls are necessary on input procedures.

Examples of typical input controls in a real-time system are as follows.

1 Access to remote input devices should be as closely controlled as is operationally feasible. Where volumes permit, the employment of a full time operator should be considered.

2 Each individual with authorised access to a remote input device must have a personal and unique code number. Some input terminals, particularly those used in factories, require the insertion of a plastic identity card bearing personal details before transmission can take place. Whether or not these cards are in use, each transaction message should have the personal code number attached to it.

3 All transaction messages should be temporarily stored on a Journal file. This provides a means of subsequently checking at least the most current transactions.

4 Exhaustive vetting tests should be given to each input message and the computer programmed to reply at once upon an error being discovered. This gives the person at the terminal an opportunity to correct the message, if possible.

5 The protection of the queue of input messages should be ensured. This

is a software and hardware problem but is none the less essential so as to avoid losing input data.

6 Re-entry of input because of equipment failure or operator error must not cause files to be updated twice.

7 When appropriate, for instance when an enquiry is made regarding the credit status of customer account number 87351, the computer should be programmed to provide a full alphabetic description so that the enquirer is able to see if an error has been made. In the example given the computer reply could well be,

Message No.	Customer A/C No.	Customer Name	Credit Limit
759	87351	Amalgamated Equipment Ltd.	£250

Date of last enquiry	Enquirers Code
15.8.72	S.D.87

The above examples, although by no means exhaustive, provide an indication of the different problems associated with real-time and on-line systems. The general control principles described previously are still largely applicable to these newer types of system but because of their size and complexity it is considered vital that the auditor is involved with the control features of the system at the very earliest planning stage.

9.6 Auditing of computer-based systems

It is generally accepted that the principles of audit are not changed with the introduction of computer-based systems. It is clear however, that some of the methods traditionally used are likely to change and it would be true to say that the emphasis of the audit programme is likely to change considerably.

Simply stated, the aims of audit, whether related to computer-based systems or not, are as follows:

1 To verify the accuracy of all matters (operations, records and procedures) which may affect the accounts of an organisation.

2 To verify the soundness of all procedures and internal checks, particularly with regard to the prevention of fraud.

3 The detection of fraud.

4 To verify that persons taking actions or making decisions have the appropriate authority and are within their legal or delegated powers.

It is fortunate that there is a large measure of agreement between the aims of audit and that of data processing management. It is probably true to say that a considerable number of audit and control principles would be incorporated into any computer-based system without any conscious thought of the audit implications, purely because sound audit principles make sound management sense.

The essence of audit applied to computer-based systems is to ascertain that the organisation, controls, checks, procedures and documentation described in the earlier part of this chapter have been implemented and are being maintained in an efficient manner. The emphasis of the audit programme will depend on the extent to which over-all control is exercised either entirely within the data processing department (for example, by batching transaction data within the control section and thus establishing batch control totals for the first time), or whether the whole operation of the data processing department can be controlled and verified by clerically maintained controls external to the data processing department.

If the data processing department can be monitored effectively purely by external controls, then the auditors task is simplified and little or no contact is necessary with the data processing department except through the reports produced.

Rarely, however, is this possible, and it is generally necessary for the auditor to consider a good proportion of the detailed controls described previously. Perhaps because of unfamiliarity or fear of the unknown it has been known for auditors to request voluminous printouts, purely for audit purposes.

Although some audit printouts will be necessary, the demand for excessive printouts solely for audit purposes negates the aim of computer-based systems in their attempt to achieve efficient data processing.

The emphasis of auditing a computer-based system will be different from that employed in a clerical system. This is because, even though a comprehensive clerical system is instituted, continuous appraisal is required owing to deviations from the system occurring due to human errors and unofficially introduced amendments.

Although, of course, this may still occur with a computer-based system, the incidence will be less, basically because of the computer's ability to carry out the job faithfully *provided that the system and program are correct to start with.*

The audit investigation

The features of a computer audit which affect all applications in the organisation are that the administrative and development controls, described previously, have been properly designed, implemented and are fully operational. The auditor should verify by observation, or on a depth-test basis, that adequate divisions of responsibilities exist, rotation of critical duties takes place, that there is proper security over the storage and access to files and programs, and that there is no unauthorised access to the computer room. The features of development controls, which were explained previously, should be checked to ensure that standardised procedures exist, and are adhered to for the initial documentation, alteration and maintenance of all stages from system design to program testing and acceptance for operational work.

The administrative and development controls serve as a framework for each job. If the general administrative and development controls are considered to be soundly based the individual job can then be examined. If one is contemplating the purchase of a house one does not examine the condition of the internal decoration before establishing that the district is acceptable and that the structure of the house is sound.

In time the auditor should develop Audit Review Questionnaires specific to each application. The generalised Review Questionnaire [16] is an excellent base from which to develop specific questionnaires to cover each of the various applications that require auditing.

The main areas of test with which the auditor will be concerned are as follows.

Input/output controls

The auditor will ascertain where in the system the control is established over batches, and thus where the emphasis of his approach must lie. Control may be first established either external to or within the data processing department. The closer to this department that control is established, the more important are the data processing department's administrative controls, and also the controls and checks incorporated in the programs.

The controls over the flow of documentation from external departments to the data processing department, the coding and preparation of data, the authorisation of amendments and transaction data should be reviewed so as to ensure that the controls are at least of the standard previously discussed.

In general, the auditor is concerned with completeness and accuracy, i.e. *all* valid data is processed and *only* valid data is processed. Where possible the computer should be programmed to anticipate each transaction and detect missing data items. The closer to the point of origin that checks are incorporated or totals are established, the more effective the control is likely to be.

File controls

If a new application is to be audited, particular care is necessary to verify that file conversion (see Section 6.3) has been carried out correctly. File conversion involves the transference of data from the records used in the previous clerical system to the computer files held on magnetic tape or disks. Invariably this involves gathering data from a number of sources and the auditor should ensure that at least the following steps have been taken. The conversion procedures and objectives should have been planned and included in the systems specification. Specific staff should be delegated for this important task and all data channelled through this section. Special conversion programs should be written incorporating as many checks on the incoming data as possible. The reference or standing data, e.g. customer's addresses, may be difficult or impossible to check by program so the auditor will wish to know what checks were made on such data. The auditor will also require to know how many rejections were discovered on the first reading of the data to be converted, how were these rejections dealt with and whether they were all re-input?

The considerable emphasis that must be given to file conversion is typical of the general emphasis of auditing computer-based systems. That is to say, more time should be spent investigating the initial stages of a job, such as the systems investigation, programming, file conversion and so on, because if the system is established correctly initially, there is a high probability that it will continue to function correctly.

If file conversion has taken place satisfactorily, the auditor should make checks on file control on a continuing basis. These checks include the following:

1 What controls ensure that only authorised amendments are processed and that all amendments are processed?
2 What controls are there to ensure that new accounts or records are not added, or that old records are not deleted without correct authorisation?
3 What control totals exist on each file, within each section of the file or within each record?
4 How are the controls in (3) verified? How often?
5 Is the standing data on each file verified? By what means?
6 What safeguards exist to ensure that the most current file is used for processing and that no wanted files are overwritten?

In addition there will be specific checks for each application which would be included in the Review Questionnaire.

Treatment of error and exceptional conditions

Most systems cater adequately for the main flow of normal items. The real test is what happens when an incorrect or exceptional item or group of items is presented to the system.

It is vital that the auditor should check the ability of each facet of the whole system (whether clerical or computer) to detect and report error and exceptional conditions.

The types of errors possible are very numerous and range from errors on single items, such as an incorrect check digit on the key, to errors on groups of items, such as an incorrect batch total.

The auditor should check carefully what procedures exist to deal with error conditions when discovered and, in particular, the procedure for ensuring that all items which were the subject of an error report are resubmitted after correction. Ideally, this part of the procedure should be computer controlled so that the machine automatically progresses the resubmission.

An exception condition, that is the one which is abnormal but not necessarily incorrect, would usually be detected by programmed checks.

The auditor is well advised to check the incidence of exception reports and, on a sample basis, establish what action is taken to deal with each of the exceptions reported. In some circumstances the exception report is merely for information but sometimes managerial action is required, followed by the input to the system of the results of such action. If the incidence of exception reports of one particular type is high this may be a pointer to some flaw in the system or, at the very least, it may indicate that re-appraisal is necessary of what constitutes an exceptional condition.

Audit trails

A feature which on occasions causes problems in the audit of d.p. systems is the partial or, more rarely, the complete loss of an audit trail in the conventional sense. With most clerical and mechanised (non-computer) systems an audit trail is an automatic by-product but this is not so with most d.p. systems. A possible way out of this problem is to insist on listings being produced of all transactions purely for audit purposes. This would clearly be highly unpopular with clients and is therefore not practicable in most cases.

The auditor must however, check that there is some method of identifying the file records and data items involved in the production of an output report or of a total. The auditor may do this by checking that each data item can be readily identified, perhaps by a unique number, studying the system specification and flowcharts and the use of test packs (see Section 9.7). He must be sure that adequate program controls exist to check that all data is dealt with, incorrect data is rejected and that all conclusions are properly based.

9.7 Tools of the computer audit

For the majority of time in carrying out the audit of a computer based system the auditor will use conventional auditing techniques such as review questionnaires, interviewing, vouching of individual transactions, reconciliation of control totals, depth checks, authorisation checks etc., but because of the nature of computer processing and recording other techniques will have a place in the auditor's armoury. A very real difficulty for the auditor is to check the contents of computer files held on magnetic storage, and to probe the workings of individual programs. To overcome these difficulties the auditors must utilise the computer itself, and two techniques which have been developed are the use of 'test packs' and the use of file interrogation programs.

Test packs

Test packs comprise representative items of test data which are processed by the operational programs in the same way as actual transaction data. The test data may be prepared by the auditor or may be selected by the auditor from the client's actual data. The aims of the test pack are to test the working of the computer program with regard to the checks on individual items. For example, does the program identify an incomplete transaction item or an incorrect check digit, and also the verification of computer produced totals? It is normal to compare the program-produced results with results that the auditor has previously calculated from the same test data.

Ideally the auditor develops test packs for each application to be audited, but there are a number of problems involved in the development of this approach to the audit. The establishment of a searching test pack takes a considerable time and involves fairly detailed knowledge of data processing. If file structures are changed and/or substantial changes to the programs are made then the test pack may be inappropriate. In spite of these disadvantages the use of test packs is likely to grow because of their undoubted value in probing the workings of programs and the speed with which checks can be made—once the test pack has been set up!

File interrogation programs

File interrogation programs are programs written so that the contents of a file, or selected facets of a file, can be examined. The programs are of a generalised nature, i.e. not specific to one application, and usually involve the auditor specifying what particular aspects of the file he wishes to examine, whereupon the file is scanned by the interrogation program and appropriate listings made. For example, if an audit enquiry was to be held concerning a computer held file containing details of personal accounts, the auditor might specify, through the use of parameter cards, that the following interrogations and listings were to be made.

1 All accounts with an adjustment exceeding £50.
2 All accounts which have had credit notes posted exceeding £20.
3 All accounts where the credit limit was not exceeded but which contained items over 3 months old.
4 A random sample of one account in every 200.
5 Various control totals to be calculated for verification with those produced by the operational programs.

Some of the file interrogation programs are written by the organisation, some are written by the computer manufacturers whilst others are written, or commissioned, by professional auditing firms. A typical example of the latter has been developed by staff of Thomson McLintock and Whinney Murray and is called ASK 360 [17].

Chapter 10   Packages and Further Accounting Applications of Computers

By now readers should have a sound knowledge of basic data processing principles and applications. Because of the importance of the foundation applications in an organisation; ledgers, costing and the like, these have been stressed most strongly in the earlier chapters. These types of applications are by no means the limit of d.p. systems and to round off this study of data processing by the accountant, some examples of more sophisticated applications are described in this chapter.

Also, there has been the general implication that all data processing applications are designed specifically for one organisation and by the staff of that organisation. This is generally true, but an alternative does exist in the form of 'packages'.

10.1   What are packages?

Various terms exist to describe packages—application packages, application software, standard systems or software packages. Regardless of the terminology used, what is being considered is a package of facilities and services that is designed to cope with some commercial job, e.g. stock control, parts explosion, payroll, etc. Technical packages, covering such matters as design and stress calculations, also exist but these are outside the scope of this book.

Typically, a commercial application package consists of a program or suite of programs, program documentation, user's manuals, instruction booklets, implementation assistance and possibly some formal tuition in the use of the package. The underlying theme of all packages is to provide a more or less ready made system that will cope with individual user's problems.

Packages are available from the computer manufacturers, specialist software houses, data processing consultants, computer bureaux or ordinary users who are capitalising on hard-won expertise. The sources of packages and of information about packages, is dealt with in greater detail in Section 10.3.

The concept of packages seems first class, that is, to spread the development costs over a number of users and to enable users to become operational that much more quickly, but there are problems. To be usable by a variety of organisations, packages have to be designed in a generalised manner. They must be able to handle many more situation types of input and output, and processing requirements than any one user would probably ever need. This tends to make them complicated and difficult to use; at least initially. A more serious problem is the uniqueness of some aspect of the organisation's activities which may not be covered by the package.

Nevertheless, if a package can be found that suits some application it may be an excellent proposition, both financially and operationally.

10.2   Assessing a package

To make a realistic appraisal of the suitability of a package is a lengthy process but even so, takes far less time than the investigation, design, programming, and implementation of a tailor-made system.

The following steps are necessary.

1 Determine the reporting facilities and routine outputs necessary to meet the organisation's requirements.

2 Determine the types and formats of the inputs available within the organisation.

3 Determine all relevant volumes (transactions, reports, outputs, amendments) currently and for the future. (Steps 1 to 3 are normal in any systems investigation and design, whether or not packages are being considered.)

4 Determine *essential* requirements and *useful* additional facilities.

5 Consider packages available (see Section 10.3) and assess suitability for the application being considered. (The assessment of the package is covered in steps 6–13.)

6 COVERAGE—What is the general coverage of the package? Is it for a very narrow area of the organisations activities or does it encompass many functions?

7 FLEXIBILITY—Is the package capable of revision and modification without substantial difficulty? Are a number of exits provided from the standard package for users to create their own additions? Can different reports be generated on demand or the reporting requirements easily inserted into the package?

8 RESTRICTIONS—What restrictions on coding, input formats, the organisation clerical systems, will be caused by the use of the package? What information, if any, will have to be foregone?

9 ASSISTANCE—Is full documentation of all aspects of the package provided? What on-site assistance is given during the implementation of the package? Is any formal training given in the use of package?

10 RELIABILITY—What is the source of the package? What do existing users, if any, say about the package itself and the supplier? If the package is not yet developed, what is the record of the package suppliers? Do they have a record of producing high quality, tested material to a definite schedule?

11 HARDWARE REQUIREMENTS—What are the core/peripheral/software requirements of the package? Can you use it on your installation?

12 PERFORMANCE—How well does package perform? What timings are available? Is a bench mark test possible? What do existing users say about performance? If package is being developed, does the specification include anticipated performance details?

13 COSTS—Will the package be paid for by outright purchase, lease or by some form of usage charge? How do the costs compare with alternative packages? How do the costs compare with the projected costs of developing a tailor-made system?

In general therefore, packages can be worthwhile in three situations.

1 Where an existing proven package more or less exactly fits the requirements of one of the organisation's applications and is a cost effective proposition.

2 Where an organisation is a new computer user and personnel of all levels are unfamiliar with data processing then the interim use of packages may be beneficial. Such use will help the organisation gain data processing expertise and refine their requirements' definitions without massive expenditure. Also, the installation is likely to become productive more quickly.

3 The third situation is where an organisation has many of the basic foundation applications operational, using tailor-made systems but wishes to develop the use of more sophisticated techniques. The use of many of these techniques (e.g. linear programming, simulation, PERT) is likely to be only occasional and a package may be the ideal answer, either on the organisation's own computer or at a bureaux.

10.3   What packages are available?

This section does not attempt to provide an exhaustive list of packages and package suppliers. Any such attempt would be out of date as soon as it was written.

However, some guidance is given to sources of information about packages and package suppliers and this will provide the starting point of the search for the most appropriate package.

Packages exist to deal with, inter alia, the following commercial jobs:

Sales and purchase accounting, invoicing, payroll, inventory management, budgetary control, costing, analyses of all types, parts explosion, scheduling, machine loading, forecasting, financial planning, portfolio management, share registration, project control, computer management, audit interrogation, incomplete records, simulation, network analysis, investment appraisal, and linear programming,

as well as a wide variety of technical, scientific and statistical applications.

Information regarding packages can be obtained initially from three main sources—organisations and associations, books, and journals—in addition, of course, to the manufacturer of the organisation's computer.

Organisations and associations

The following organisations have an interest in the supply or use of packages.

Computer Services and Bureaux Association (COSBA),
    Leicester House, 8 Liecester Street, London WC2.
COPAC Index,
    RAC House, Landsdowne Road, Croydon.
National Computing Centre (NCC),
    Quay House, Quay Street, Manchester 3.
Software Houses Association,
    109 Kingsway, London WC2.

Books

The NCC made a valiant attempt to survey the whole field of commercial packages by the publication of 'Computer Application Packages' in 1968. Although now out of date, the book has much valuable information on the use of packages as well as the packages then available.

A book by one of the present co-authors gives a brief description of the scope and contents of 50 commercial packages, as well as the names of the suppliers [10].

Journals

There are a number of journals and publications covering the field of data processing. These include: *Data Processing*, *Data Systems*, *Data Week*, *Computer Weekly* and the British Computer Society Publications—*Computer Journal* and *Computer Bulletin*. These publications carry advertisements for packages and from time to time include special features about all aspects of data processing, including packages. An excellent example of the latter was the special supplement in *Data Processing* [18]. Apart from articles about packages, the supplement gave a table of 44 suppliers of packages, the packages that were available, and brief details of hardware requirements, price, and ancillary services.

The above sources of information will help to track down likely package suppliers from whom can be obtained the detailed information necessary to carry out the assessment discussed in Section 10.2.

To summarise: before your organisation embarks on the development of a tailor-made system, are you sure that no package exists that will cope with the work? When one considers how many people have independently, and expensively, solved the same problems in sales accounting, credit control, rates accounting and the like, it is enough to make any accountant shudder.

10.4 Mathematical and statistical techniques

In recent years increasing attention, particularly in academic circles, has been given to the use of mathematical and statistical techniques for solving accounting problems. It is apparent that practice has lagged considerably behind theory in this area yet the situation is changing, and one recognition of this change is the inclusion of papers covering analytical techniques in the examinations of the main accounting bodies. It is no coincidence that the growth of interest in, and the use of, such techniques has run parallel with the development of computers. To solve many practical problems, within a sensible time and cost, virtually demands the use of a computer.

For all accountants, but particularly those concerned with the provision of planning, control, and decision making information, the newer techniques provide exciting extensions to their skills. To round-off this book a brief description of some of the accounting applications of mathematical and statistical techniques will be given, together with a number of references for readers wishing to pursue the subject.

10.5 Models and model building

Underlying most of the applications of mathematical and statistical techniques are the concepts of models and model building.

A model, simply, is any representation of real life or real life situation in a numeric, financial or verbal form. From this definition it is apparent that balance sheets, costing statements, and indeed the whole double entry system, are models, and thus accountants have been dealing with models, albeit unwittingly, for generations.

However, these types of models are largely descriptive. That is, they give a simplified description of a situation for a given period or at a given point in time. Comparatively little attempt has been made to show and depict the underlying factors, interactions, and relationships which produce the particular results shown on the accounting statements produced. Of course, some aspects of accounting do attempt the identification of the underlying relationships. An example of this is cost/volume/profit analysis where interactions between fixed and variable costs, contribution, and volume, are studied.

More sophisticated models which do attempt to depict the underlying relationships can be termed analytical models and have the great advantage over descriptive models of being capable of being used as predictors. The predictive element of analytical models is the main reason for their construction and attempts to answer the question, 'What will happen if . . . ?'

10.6   Model formulation

Although the problems being considered vary widely, and the resulting models have often no apparent relationship there is a general pattern in their method of construction. Such a pattern is shown in Fig. 10.1. One of the main advan-

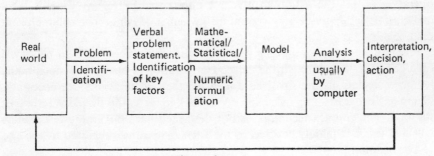

FIG. 10.1   Steps in model construction and use

tages in going beyond merely a verbal statement of the problem is that when a problem is put into a mathematical and statistical form, analysis is possible and alternatives can be considered.

Alas, Utopia is not yet at hand and several problems remain. The world of mathematical models is orderly, simple, and logical yet, unfortunately, the real world is complex, disordered and sometimes illogical. The problem that the model builder has is to identify the critical factors for inclusion in the model. Not all real life factors can or should be included in the model, and the real skill lies in deciding what are the appropriate variables and their relationships, and not in the manipulation of these factors by the computer.

Furthermore, there is no way of *proving* that the model will give an accurate representation of real life. It is necessary for any result to be examined to see if it is feasible and realistic. The process of model building is an interative one. First attempts are crude and many important factors are incorrect or omitted. The refinement of the model is not only useful in its own right but also for the insight it can give management into what are the critical factors in any situation.

From the earlier definition of model it is apparent that a very wide variety of models exist. Many are unique to a particular situation or organisation, whilst others have a more or less similar structure. An example of a fairly standard type of model is that of linear programming.

10.7   Linear programming

Linear programming is one of the most successfully applied mathematical techniques and has many applications. It is an optimising technique which can be used to indicate the best way to achieve some desired objective, e.g. maximum profit or minimum cost, whilst keeping within certain constraints on the amounts of resources available, e.g. production time, labour or materials.

Linear programming deals with linear relationships, e.g. a doubling of output will take twice the production hours. Clearly, the assumption of strict proportionality is not true for all levels of activity but over the feasible operating ranges the assumption is not unreasonable. In any case, it is an assumption often made by accountants when analysing cost/volume/profit relationships.

Practical linear programming problems virtually always need to be solved on a computer as, although the method of solution is basically simple, many tedious calculations are involved and a number of iterations are necessary. Computer programs use a variant of what is known as the simplex method of solution. The simplex technique is not described here but interested readers will find this adequately covered in the further reading suggested at the end of this chapter.

Linear programming can be a very useful tool where the appropriate conditions exist, i.e. where linear objectives are to be optimised within linear constraints. The accountant's main tasks are to recognise where such conditions exist—or can be assumed to exist—and to supply the required marginal contribution figures, rates of usage of resources, and resource limitations.

10.8   Linear programming and cost/volume/profit analysis

In cost/volume/profit analysis, linearity of variable costs and contribution is generally assumed and often a given product mix. In some simple cases, the analysis is of use in deciding what is the best product mix. In this context 'best' is taken to mean maximum contribution.

Consider the situation where a firm, with fixed costs of £200,000, produces and sells two products, X and Y. The relevant data is as follows:

	Product X	Product Y
Per cwt	£	£
Selling price	10	8
Marginal cost	5	6
Contribution	5	2
Contribution/sales ratio	50%	25%

The assumed sales and production ratio is 2X:1Y.

Using this information the anticipated profit at any level of sales can be read from a profit graph such as Fig. 10.2.

However, as the sales ratio changes the anticipated profit also changes. Various other sales ratios are given in Fig. 10.2b.

The above illustration is clearly unrealistically simple. It does not include any constraints and begs what is probably the most important question. What is the most profitab'e product combination to aim for? It does show however the effects on profit of varying the sales mix.

Assume that the products X and Y can be produced with identical facilities and that there are 400,000 production hours available. One cwt of X takes 4 hours and one cwt of Y takes 1 hour. What is now the most profitable product or product combination? Normally the contribution per unit of the limiting factor (constraint) is calculated thus—

	Product X	Product Y
	£	£
Contribution per cwt	5	2
Production hours per cwt	4	1
Contribution per hour	1.25	2

The product with the highest contribution per unit of the limiting factor would be preferred. In this case, assuming no other constraints, Y would be preferred and X would never be produced.

In situations where there are few products and few constraints, the contribution per unit of the limiting factor approach may be satisfactory but for virtually any real life product combination problem it is inadequate.

Continuing the above illustration assume that a third product, Z, is introduced with a selling price of £9 per cwt and a marginal cost of £6 per cwt. Assume also that all products have now to undergo a two stage process (production and grading) and that there are certain sales limitations. The full data is set out below.

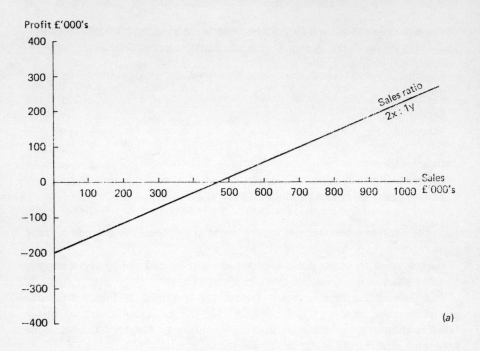

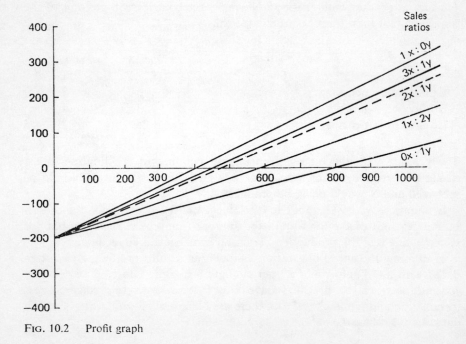

Fig. 10.2   Profit graph

	Product X	Product Y	Product Z
Selling price/cwt	£10	£8	£9
Marginal cost/cwt	£5	£6	£6
Production time/cwt	4 hr	1 hr	2 hr
Grading time/cwt	1 hr	2 hr	2 hr
Maximum sales possible (cwt)	50,000	100,000	50,000

The total production time available is 400,000 hours and the total grading time 200,000 hours. Fixed costs are expected to remain at £200,000 and the objective is choose the production combination that will maximise profitability.

The above case, although much smaller than real situations, is already very cumbersome to solve by conventional accounting means. It is, however, easily soluble by linear programming and because of its very small size can be solved manually in a few minutes although larger problems need the help of a computer.

The basic linear programming formulation is as shown in Fig. 10.3 together with the optimum solution.

Basic formulation

Contribution

$$5x + 2y + 3z = C$$

Production restrictions

$$4x + 1y + 2z \leqslant 400,000 \quad \text{(production)}$$
$$1x + 2y + 2z \leqslant 200,000 \quad \text{(grading)}$$

Sales restrictions

$$1x \qquad\qquad \leqslant 50,000$$
$$1y \qquad\qquad <100,000$$
$$1z \qquad\quad \leqslant 50,000$$

Objective: Maximise C where X, Y, Z, are production in cwts of the respective products

Solution

$$c = £450,000 \therefore \text{profit} = £250,000$$
when $x = $ 50,000 cwt
$y = $ 25,000 cwt
$z = $ 50,000 cwt
325,000 production hours used
200,000 grading hours used

FIG. 10.3   Basic linear programming formulation and solution

From this solution it will be noted that all the grading time has been used but there are 75,000 spare production hours.

The usefulness of linear programming is not limited merely to the calculation of the optimum solution, and some other features which are of interest to accountants are as follows.

Shadow prices

Shadow prices, or alternatively dual evaluators, are the opportunity costs of scarce resources. If a resource is not totally used in the optimum plan its opportunity cost is zero. Shadow prices are an automatic by-product of the simplex method of solution and provide some guide to the marginal value of additional units of constraints. For example, in the illustration shown in Fig. 10.3 the increase in contribution resulting from marginal increments of constraints are as follows:

Raising of constraint	*Increase of contribution per unit of constraint*
	£
Production hours	0*
Grading hours	1
Sales of X	4
Sales of Y	0*
Sales of Z	1

* The opportunity cost of these constraints is zero because the limit of the constraint had not been reached in the optimum solution, so increasing the limit of the constraint will not increase contribution.

The shadow prices produced by the linear programming model are not prepared in accounting systems, yet for a number of purposes they are probably the most relevant figures that could be produced.

The shadow prices produced by the model are only appropriate for specified ranges of contribution margins, capacities, and production coefficients, and thus appropriate changes in coefficients will automatically produce new shadow prices reflecting the changed conditions.

Sensitivity analysis

Models and plans are based on data which is subject to variation, and management are concerned to know the effects of changing conditions, values, and prices on the original plan. What is termed 'sensitivity analysis' can assist management in this aim.

The coefficients used in linear programming, e.g. the £5 contribution for product X, the 2 hours grading time for product Z, etc., in the earlier illustration, are usually an average or a best-estimate value. Because of this it is useful to consider the sensitivity of the optimum solution to variations in the coefficients.

In a given situation a slight change in a coefficient, e.g. rate of production, may result in a new solution with a substantial change in profitability. For other coefficients, relatively large changes may result in little or no change in profitability.

Using most linear programming computer packages, the sensitivity of the model can be explored by varying any of the coefficients or by adding or eliminating constraints. Most computer linear programming packages supply the range on each side of specified coefficients within which the original optimum solution will still apply.

A simple example, again based on the illustration in Fig. 10.3, might be to consider the effects of a change in the grading hours for product X, from 1 hour to 2 hours. This particular change results in a different solution (as it obviously should with such a large relative change), as follows:

Contribution   £400,000 ∴ profit £200,000
Product X   £50,000   cwt production
Product Y   nil   cwt production
Product Z   £50,000   cwt production
300,000 production hours used
200,000 grading hours used

Linear programming has many applications and the following are examples of its use in areas of particular interest to accountants:

Resource allocation.
Capital budgeting.
Variance analysis (using shadow prices).
Budgeting and financial planning.
Cost allocations.
In conjunction with critical path analysis.
Transportation and location problems.
Material utilisation, mixes and blends.

No attempt at rigour has been made in the above section on linear programming and many technical points have been omitted. However, it is hoped that it will encourage some readers to develop their knowledge further by studying some of the references at the end of this chapter.

10.9   Simulation

A technique which is even more dependent on the use of a computer is simulation. Some problems are not suitable for analytical techniques, such as linear programming, because they may be too cumbersome or complex to solve or the data may not all be available. In such cases simulation could be the answer.

The essential characteristic of simulation is the setting up of a numerical model that represents the structure of a system, and then manipulating the model to represent the behaviour of the system being studied over a period of time. Time is the essential element of simulation and a simulation representing many weeks operation of say, an inventory control system, may be done in a matter of minutes on a computer. In most cases, simulation models do not produce optimum solutions. They represent what will happen if a system is set up in a certain way with differing values of variables and relationships.

Many systems which are simulated involve random or probabilistic elements, e.g. arrivals of customers at a service point, so the simulation model must provide for this variability. This is usually done by the Monte-Carlo method. This is a technique for selecting numbers randomly from probability distributions for use in a particular run of the model. In this way the probabilistic features inherent in the physical system are reflected in the numeric model.

The construction of simulation models does not necessarily involve sophisticated mathematics, but it does require a thorough knowledge of the critical factors and relationships in a real system. An incidental advantage of any model building is the insight it gives into the working of the physical system.

Realistic simulation is totally dependent on the computer and the use of simulation in business did not really start until the advent of the computer. Simulation has been used for total firm simulation, e.g. the development of the Industrial Dynamics model by Forrester and the budget model of the firm by Mattessich, or parts of the total business system, e.g. inventory systems, queueing systems and risk analysis in capital budgeting.

A useful way for the accountant to gain some experience in simulation and model building is to use one of the financial planning packages that are available.

An example is the PROSPER (PROfit Simulation, Planning and Evaluation of Risk) package developed by ICL. This package is extremely flexible and covers; profit projections, project profitability, risk evaluation, cash flow analyses, comparisons of alternative strategies, costing models, cost/volume/ profit analysis and forecasting. The use of such a package may help to indicate ways in which models could be developed specifically related to the accountant's own organisation.

10-10 Further reading

BATTERSBY, A., *Mathematics in management*, Penguin (1966).

CORCORAN, A. W., *Mathematical applications in accounting*, Harcourt, Brace and World (1968).

LIVINGSTONE, J. L. (Editor), *Management planning and control*, McGraw-Hill (1970). Regardless of its title, this book contains a series of articles on the application of mathematical and statistical techniques to accounting. It also contains a wealth of additional references.

MATTESSICH, R., *Simulation of the firm through a budget computer program*, Irwin (1964).

MEIER, R. C., NEWELL, W. T. and PAZER, H. L., *Simulation in business economics*, Prentice-Hall (1969).

MORISON, A., BURDEN, R. and CRABTREE, H., *Understanding modern business mathematics*, Scottish Institute of Chartered Accountants (1971).

STAFFORD, L. W. T., *Business mathematics*, Macdonald and Evans (1969).

PROSPER manual, ICL (1970).

References

1 *Getting the most out of your computer*, McKinsey (1968).

2 *Unlocking the computer's profit potential*, McKinsey (1968).

3 *Computers in Sheffield—a sample study*, P.E. Consulting Group (1971).

4 *Management information systems and the computer*, Parts I and II, Institute of Cost and Works Accountants (1967, 1969).

5 *Internal control in a computer-based accounting system*, Institute of Chartered Accountants (1969).

6 *The audit of computer-based accounting systems*, Institute of Chartered Accountants 1969).

7 'A survey of computer usage', *Management Accounting* (June 1969).

8 BRIDGMAN and GREEN, *ibid.* (December 1966).

9 BRINJES, J. S., *The Accountant* (29 October 1970).

10 CLIFTON, H. D., *Systems analysis for business data processing*, Business Books (Second edition, 1972).

11 SMYTHE, *Guide to computer input preparation*, Business Publications (1970).

12 CLIFTON, H. D., *Data processing systems design*, Business Books (1971).

13 MERRETT, A. J. and SYKES, A., *Capital budgeting and company finance*, Longmans (1969).

14 BRANDON, D. H., *Management standards for data processing*, Van Nostrand (1963).

15 *'PAC I' project control system*, John Hoskyns and Company, Limited.

16 *Statements on auditing–appendix*, Institute of Chartered Accountants.

17 CRABTREE, M. G. and OAKLEY, A., 'An interrogation kit', *Accountancy*, Vol. LXXX, No. 915 (November 1969).

18 'Supplement—software packages', *Data Processing* (November/December, 1970).

Index